Groups
and individuals:
explanations in
social psychology

Groups
and individuals:
explanations in
social psychology

WILLEM DOISE
Professor of Experimental Social Psychology
University of Geneva

TRANSLATED BY DOUGLAS GRAHAM
Senior Lecturer in Psychology
University of Durham

CAMBRIDGE UNIVERSITY PRESS
Cambridge London New York Melbourne

Published by the Syndics of the Cambridge University Press
The Pitt Building, Trumpington Street, Cambridge CB2 1RP
Bentley House, 200 Euston Road, London NW1 2DB
32 East 57th Street, New York, NY 10022, USA
296 Beaconsfield Parade, Middle Park, Melbourne 3206, Australia

French edition © Editions A. De Boeck, Brussels, 1976

© Cambridge University Press 1978

L'Articulation psychosociologique et les relations entre groupes first published by
A. De Boeck, Brussels, 1976

English translation first published by the Cambridge University Press 1978

Printed in Great Britain at the University Press, Cambridge

Library of Congress Cataloguing in Publication Data
Doise, Willem.
Groups and individuals.
Translation of L'articulation psychosociologique et les relations entre groupes.
Bibliography: p.
Includes index.
1. Interpersonal relations. 2. Social psychology.
I. Title.
HM132.D6513   301.11   77-84800

ISBN 0 521 21953 1 hard covers
ISBN 0 521 29320 0 paperback

Contents

Contents

Acknowledgements

The author and publisher are grateful to the following for permission to reproduce copyright material:
Table 1 Copyright 1966 by Duke University Press
Table 9 Copyright 1957 by the American Psychological Association. Reprinted by permission
Table 10 Copyright 1971 by the American Psychological Association. Reprinted by permission
Figure 8 Cambridge University Press

Foreword to the English edition

The publication in English of Willem Doise's book should be seen against the background of recent controversies in social psychology. The strength of the discipline and the main feature distinguishing it from other social sciences were traditionally seen in its use of experimental methods of research. The aim was, some forty years ago, to create a reliably scientific approach to human social behaviour. This developed in due course into experimental social psychology which overwhelmingly dominated (and still does) the research and writing in the subject. But what started as an exciting new venture became over the years, as is often the case, a complacent and unquestioned old routine. It is therefore not surprising that the 'experimental' tradition found itself at the receiving end of most of the attacks directed in the last ten years or so at the *kind* of research done by social psychologists.

These criticisms came from many different quarters and took many different forms. It has always been my view that to attack a method of conducting research for reasons other than the demonstrable weaknesses of its internal logic is a waste of time. It is obvious that social psychological experiments have their weaknesses *because* they are experiments, and I shall not attempt to rehearse here the well-known litany of complaints. It is just as obvious that social psychological experiments have their strengths *because* they are experiments, and once again, this is not the place for an enumeration of well-known and platitudinous truths. Willem Doise in this book leaves far behind him this well-worn and vacuous controversy in which the height of passions has certainly not been matched by any worthwhile new research developments. Doise is concerned with a more important issue which really *is* worth discussing: the nature and range of theories underlying research, experimental or any other. But – as distinct from some of the critics who seem to continue for ever the gratifying contemplation of their own vast and 'programmatic' statements – he leads us directly from a general discussion about social psychology into studies which explore exciting areas of new knowledge.

Doise's general discussion remains firmly within a framework which has recently become important to many of us, on both sides of the Atlantic. It is concerned with bringing social psychology back into society while maintaining at the same time its links with general psychological theory. His book is one of the attempts to get the best of these two worlds which have often been at odds with one another. The merit of the book is that it takes one step forward in providing *through research* a new 'context for social psychology' – a context which has to do with human sociality *and* human society at the same time.

It is appropriate that the studies on the relationships between cognitive development and social interaction, described in Chapter 3, should have emerged directly from the Piagetian *sanctum*. The links between the individual and the 'collective' structuring of cognitive experience have preoccupied Piaget for a long time although they were never given much prominence in the enormous amount of research which came out of Geneva. And yet, Piaget was clearly led to this theoretical borderline when he wrote, between 1941 and 1950, the essays published together in 1965 under the title of *Etudes sociologiques*, and even today still not available in an English translation.

Willem Doise describes in this book the beginnings of the new research on the role of social interaction in the children's achievement of certain Piagetian 'operations', and this kind of work is continuing at present in Geneva under his direction. It consists, in a sense, of actively bringing the sociality of a 'group' into the study of cognitive functioning. In the later sections of the book the range widens from a 'group' or an 'ingroup' to relations between social groups – and this is where 'sociality' merges into society. But the argument – and the studies reported in the book – remain firmly planted in the social psychological theory of certain cognitive processes which are crucial to the active human structuring of the social environment. One of the points of departure is found in some of my earlier work, in the late 1950s and early 1960s, on the processes of social categorisation and their role in organising our attitudes and behaviour towards our own social group and other groups. But while this initial analysis was mainly concerned with certain cognitive and 'value' aspects of social categorisations, Willem Doise once again widens the range. He argues for the essential unity of the categorising process in its capacity to determine simultaneously the structure of cognitions, the system of values and the modes of behaviour as they all relate to the segmentation of each human society into distinct social groups.

The background of it all comes from social psychology, social anthropology and sociology. New evidence comes from several studies recently conducted in Geneva and elsewhere, and described in the book. I cannot resist the temptation of mentioning that Doise missed in his book a richly rewarding empirical example of the cognitive–evaluative–behavioural unity for which he argues – but it is only fair to add that it would have been almost impossible for him to know anything about it. There was a time in north Oxford, in the mid-1930s, when a newly built working-class council estate had a direct border with a middle-class 'urban housing estate'. A protracted battle developed to establish a clear separation between the two, and finally the inhabitants of the urban estate managed to have a high wall erected in the middle of a street so that the twain should never be able to meet. My old friend and colleague from our Oxford days, Peter Collison, described this epic struggle in *The Cutteslowe Walls*, published in 1963. The walls did not finally come down until 1959. They undoubtedly represented an unexplored architectural (and therefore behavioural) addition to Doise's unitary perspective of category divisions.

It only remains for me to add that, despite the Cutteslowe walls, I am not fully convinced by the *sufficiency* of Doise's unitary argument, although I have no doubt that the establishment of social categorisations of a certain kind is a *necessary* condition for the appearance of some forms of collective social behaviour. The forms of social category differentiations which some of us began discussing twenty years ago were deeply rooted in the contemporary developments of cognitive theory – mainly as they were represented by the work done at the time by Jerome Bruner. The problem still remained – for a social psychologist – how to insert these cognitive processes into various frameworks and forms of social reality. This turned out to be a long-lasting job which took us well into the 1970s. But this is a lengthy story which has been discussed elsewhere, and will undoubtedly continue on its stumbling progression. The fundamentally important thing about Willem Doise's work, as it is represented in this book, is that it places itself squarely at the focus of what is a crucial new hope for a further development of social psychology. Social behaviour seen in the wide context of social reality cannot be understood without going back to some forms of cognitive theory which are appropriate for our purposes. But this work must also be done with genuine sensitivity to the nature of the wider social structures inside which we perceive, think, create and categorise. Through the width of his interests and his intellectual background, Doise is one of the people who can provide the beginnings of this new synthesis. This is clearly demonstrated in the contents of this book.

HENRI TAJFEL

Preface

For some years, social psychology has been in a state of uncertainty. After so many 'certainties', significant discoveries, definition of fields of research and enthusiastic applications of findings, there is now a feeling that stock should be taken, and that there may be other directions in which research may be undertaken. This may sound rather vague, but is not without its point. Doubts come from the uncertainties within groups of scientists which are provoked by the slowing down of the process of discovery and of the contribution of new ideas and techniques. It is said that not to make progress is to fall behind, and this is especially felt in groups who are mainly concerned with innovation and progress. There is also the feeling that, by becoming involved in a particular line of action, social psychologists have neglected a major aspect of social activity, and have become bogged down in an intellectual model which has prevented them, and still prevents them, from coming to grips with such neglected aspects of social life as social change, innovation, intergroup relations, ideology, political dynamics and so on. Finally, account must be taken of new kinds of research with their own intellectual traditions and social and political preoccupations, distinct from those predominant in American social psychology. Some people may indeed be opposed to this kind of diversification, even regarding it as a threat to the universality and unity of a science which already has so many problems and is so liable to criticism. They may be right, but I do not believe they are. In fact, these points of view have initiated fresh theoretical,

xiii

ideological and political discussion. And in this discussion I can see many promising and healthy aspects. I would go so far as to regret that such discussion does not occur more frequently, since differences of this kind sow the seeds of open-mindedness and progress. So the question with regard to the future of social psychology is whether it should continue as an independent discipline, or as a part of general psychology. Since this is a real problem, we should surely discuss it openly, especially at a time like the present, a time of crisis and decision. Because if social psychology has a future other than that of cherished academic respectability, a place other than that simply assigned by a classification of science, it must change its focus and interests.

These thoughts of mine were stimulated by Willem Doise's wide-ranging and precisely written book, which I should regard as aimed at expressing and provoking just such a change. Let it be said that superficially, we have a scholarly piece of work, and let us approve its competence, which indeed deserves our respect. We also find, however, the uncertainty and doubts of the researcher, and that there is little literature relevant to the issues concerned. Intergroup relations represent the centre of the field, and we must consider questions of sociological and psychological explanation of intergroup phenomena. To start with, there is the question of the limits of explanation. To extrapolate from the individual case, even for a Lorenz, a Freud or a Piaget, is to attempt the logically impossible. To turn one's back on the relations of production, and on their ideological counterpart is not good enough either. Doise's discussion of such issues is meticulous, the contribution of each level of explanation is evaluated, and the possibility of integration outlined. Instead of having to make up our minds, as we generally have, on an arbitrarily defined basis, we have here something solid to go on. We should all be able to appreciate the discussion which leads to Doise's conclusion that the contact-point between psychological and sociological is to be found at the level of cognitive structures. We have here the bridge we are seeking. Doise combines brilliantly the notion of such cognitive structures with the development of social interaction. It is a kind of bridge which has attracted Piaget himself, although most of his followers have ignored it. In the present book, the author is not concerned with individual dispositions, but with a programme of research, manifested in a series of pioneering experiments. On the basis of results from these experiments, there would seem to be a good prospect of integrating genetic psychology and social psychology. The attempt at a rapprochement between these two branches of knowledge is based on empirical findings which provide the best kind of support. The whole of the first part of the book represents a kind of penetration into a hitherto unexplored field. In the future, we shall have to improve our understanding of the logic of social interaction before we can explain the dynamics underlying the processes involved. But we must take things as they come, and the issues raised do indicate the kinds of terms in which they may find an answer.

The second part of the book, devoted to groups and their interrelations, is more directly concerned with social psychology. The problem was approached thirty years ago and then left in limbo. The experiments here revive interest in such questions. The notion of category differentiation, which underlies these experiments, brings together both social discrimination and individual and group preferences.

These researches have been carried out within a framework under pressure both to be rigorous and to recognise the significant factors in social life. I am personally impressed by the constant concern with emotional factors which the author shows in his treatment of the subject. He seems continually to bear in mind the general importance of the principle of integration between psychology and sociology. What he says about aggression, ideology, psychogenesis and representations indicates that what is involved is the position and outlook of our own science within the context of the other psychological and social sciences. But beyond this, we need a detailed analysis and rational development of what is known on such an important issue. Each of us thinks he knows a lot. Now, we are not concerned here with 'social psychology without tears', but with a worthwhile social psychology. After reading the present book, I feel that we would be better off if we had more books like it. I am sure that every reader, however critical, will feel the same. Indeed, I hope it may benefit from that lively criticism which is surely much more valuable than the polite or indifferent acceptance with which one so commonly greets a work so demanding of time and effort. This is a book which all may read with profit.

SERGE MOSCOVICI

PART I

The integration of psychology and sociology

The social psychology of intergroup relations is well established. The purpose of the present book is to acquaint the reader with recent progress in this area of the social sciences. But social psychological experimentation has no monopoly in the study of intergroup relations. Intergroup relations also have their roots in psychology; they inevitably develop as a result of individual patterns of behaviour, and attempts have been made by psychologists to study them at the individual level. On the other hand, relations between groups always develop within a framework of social, economic, political and ideological organisations. Intergroup relations have also their sociological context.

The first two chapters of the present book will be concerned with the special features and limitations of psychological and sociological explanations in the field of group relations. We shall then try to outline a way in which these two levels may be integrated, both theoretically and experimentally. This kind of integration is precisely the concern of experimental social psychology. Examples from outside the field of intergroup relations will be given to illustrate the specific nature of this approach. The last three chapters will try to take detailed account of the results of social psychological experiments in intergroup relations.

Any conflict between two modes of explanation in the social sciences inevitably involves tensions. The present book may help to suggest why this should be so. As far as the account given of the sociological approach is concerned,

1

it will deal with the impossibility of isolating scientific activity from ideological issues.

It will also be argued that the different scientific activities are in fact transformations of each other. The inevitable consequence is friction between different scientific groups or schools. This in itself, indeed, represents a case of intergroup dynamics.

I

The psychological approach

By definition, the approaches which we regard as psychological attempt to explain in individual terms the way in which the individual is involved in the development of intergroup relations. The explanations provided are often of a historical nature. Phylogenetic or ontogenetic development is cited to account for the behaviour of individuals. A number of such approaches will be examined here.

Common sense already provides psychological explanations. A scarcely more scientific approach is based on the notion of instinct, which we find in one of the first attempts at systematic social psychology (McDougall, 1908). Lorenz (1966) has again brought forward this notion by publishing a best-seller which we shall summarise and comment upon critically, because it advances such an unsatisfactory account of certain aspects of intergroup relations. To Lorenz's devious explanation of human aggressiveness, we shall oppose a more direct study by Berkowitz (1965) concerned with factors actually present. Many writers have gone back to Freud in order to explain certain psychological aspects of intergroup relations. According to them, regression to earlier stages of development can furnish an explanation of certain kinds of social behaviour. Freud himself (1955) actually published a study of 'group behaviour' which took more account of factors in the current situation, and of which we shall also give an account. As an illustration of the ontogenetic approach we have chosen a study by Piaget and Weil (1951) which describes the psychogenesis of the notions of one's own and other countries. After these fairly well

3

structured approaches, we may profitably refer to a typical case from 'clinical psychology'. Clinical psychology uses many methods of investigation deriving from different theoretical systems. The work of Smith, Bruner and White (1956) takes advantage of both worlds by combining a clinical approach with a psychological theory of opinion. We shall finally give a brief account of our earlier research (Doise, 1969b). While essentially psychological, it is also relevant for sociology. Our interest in the integration of psychology and sociology dates from this study.

COMMONSENSE PSYCHOLOGY

Against the background of strife and warfare which has for so long represented official history, certain figures are distinguished in legends and epics. Frequently their personal characteristics, their courage or cowardice, their craft or their wrath, their sulks or their strength, are advanced as explanations of intergroup relations. Some succeed because they are brave and valiant, others fail because they are timorous and cowardly, and yet others remain out of contention because they do not fulfil their obligations to allies, or are simply idle.

These represent the tautologies of common sense. They become scientific only in so far as they become objects of reflection and transformation, as we shall see later. Professional psychologists, however, armed with a whole arsenal of statistics, often proceed in a manner scarcely less tautological. As an example of this, we may cite Rotter (1971) who, in a presidential address to a section of the American Psychological Association, put forward a scale dealing with interpersonal confidence. The test consists of 25 questions concerning the confidence which the subject has in the statements made by others. The 'others' are not particular persons but categories of persons considered to be important for the subjects. The questions have to do with the confidence accorded to teachers, students, judges, journalists and politicians. The author of the test (Rotter, 1967) has shown that the scores of student subjects on his scale substantially agree with the view that their comrades have of them. It is, however, of interest to note what happens when very trusting and very mistrustful subjects take part in different experimental situations. Roberts (1967, cited by Rotter, 1971, p. 448) has done just this. In a problem solving task, the experimenter gave certain instructions to the subjects on different trials. In the case of the first instructions, the 'trusting' and 'mistrustful' subjects, selected according to their test response, both followed the experimenter's instructions. They continued to do so while these instructions proved useful. For these subjects, therefore, the experimental situation counteracted any so-called 'personality differences'. On the other hand, however, when the instructions proved to be misleading, i.e. 'bad', the 'mistrustful' subjects stopped following them sooner than the trusting subjects. After being misled twice or three times, almost all the subjects, regardless of their previous response to the 'trust' test, stopped following the advice given. This shows how restricted Rotter's test is. For one thing, most of the differences in response between the subjects is accounted for not by the test but by the experimental situation. Useful advice is followed, advice which is not useful is not followed. On the other hand, subjects who have already declared themselves 'mistrustful' more readily reject ineffective advice than other subjects. All the test shows, therefore, is that there is some correspondence between the accounts which subjects give of their normal behaviour and their behaviour in a particular situation. This seems not far removed from the familiar commonsense tautology.

Moreover, the responses to Rotter's test themselves vary with social factors. Every year, the students in an introductory course in psychology answered Rotter's test. The following are the conclusions based on a comparison of results for different years.

In the 1964 study, the average score was 72.4; in 1969, it was 66.6. . . The difference is not only highly statistically significant, but it indicates that a student who was at the mean of the distribution in 1969 would have been in the lower one-third of the distribution in 1964 . . . An item analysis was made to discover how general was the drop in trust . . . The items that showed the greatest decrease included those in the areas of politics, peace keeping, and communications. The items that showed little or no change included mainly those dealing with social agents with whom the subjects were likely to have had some direct contact (Rotter, 1971, p. 451).

Although psychometric tools may enable us to attribute to each individual a given degree of a characteristic, they do not explain where this characteristic came from. Such tools only enable us to describe and differentiate in a more sophisticated way than does commonsense.

THE ETHOLOGICAL ILLUSION

The functioning of an individual at any given moment in his life can be understood only in terms of his current situation and his past history. The study of trust provides a clear example. Clinical and developmental psychologists base their understanding on the personal history of the individual. Such an ontogenetic account must, however, be related to a study of the origin of species. With phylogenetic development, mechanisms of adaptation and survival have also developed, and have been inherited by the human species. Thus the notion of instinct or drive has frequently been used by psychologists.

Certain ethological studies have attempted to revive this phylogenetic kind of explanation. Lorenz's book *On Aggression* represents such an attempt. The author regards the book as relevant to the study of intergroup relations. 'Humanity is not enthusiastically combative because it is split into political parties, but it is divided into opposing camps because this is the adequate stimulus situation to arouse militant enthusiasm in a satisfying manner' (Lorenz, 1966, p. 234). Before we can estimate the value of this conclusion we must see how Lorenz reached it.

The theory behind Lorenz's book is a neo-Darwinian one;

mutation and selection are described as the media of evolution. Intra-species aggression is used for the benefit of the species, ensures that members of the species have the necessary living space, provides better fathers and mothers and selectively preserves the brave defenders of the herd. Among certain species, aggression also serves to establish a social hierarchy which has 'great survival value' (ibid, p. 35).

Like feeding, sexual behaviour or flight, aggression comes into action spontaneously in the presence of certain releasers. The different instincts, however, do not govern animal behaviour independently of one another, in turn and according to their various strengths; instinctive regulators play a part. Just as, in ontogenesis, habits are acquired and become autonomous, so in the course of phylogenesis, ritualised behaviours become autonomous and transmitted by heredity. Such rituals integrate and co-ordinate very different forms of behaviour. The ritual of instigation in certain ducks exemplifies this. The female combines a threatening movement with regard to an enemy, with a movement of submission and flight toward the male. Phylogenetic rituals represent new instincts. 'By the process of phylogenetic ritualization a new and completely autonomous instinct may evolve which is, in principle, just as independent as any of the so-called "great" drives such as hunger, sex, fear or aggression, and which – like these – has its seat in the great parliament of instincts' (ibid, p. 56).

Such rituals serve as the regulators of aggression; for example, the ceremony of intimidation which enables the antagonists to gauge their strength so that later the weaker can give up the combat. Aggression is most inhibited when inter-individual ties are formed and are represented by rituals which develop only between particular individuals. The appeasement ritual of certain ducks, the dance of the cranes and the triumph ritual among geese are examples of relations exclusive to two individuals which may outlast the sexual bond and which are sometimes to be found between creatures of the same species and of the same sex. In basing his argument on the two-fold nature of these rituals, i.e. an impulse of aggression toward a third party redirected into an impulse of approach toward the partner, Lorenz (ibid, p. 184) does not hesitate to conclude that 'in every case of genuine love there is a high measure of latent aggression, normally obscured by the bond, that on the rupturing of this bond the horrible phenomenon known as hate makes its appearance. There is no love without aggression, but there is no hate without love.'

This last quotation prepares us for a sermon on the condition of man. In the penultimate chapter, entitled 'Ecce Homo', man is, in fact, compared to a dove, a rather aggressive bird, which, by an accident of nature, suddenly finds itself possessed of the beak of a crow. According to Lorenz, the condition of the human race is characterised by the disequilibrium involved in the fact that, on the one hand, it has very powerful artificial tools of aggression, while on the other hand, it lacks artificial regulators to match them. Moreover, man's command of the non-human environment being virtually unassailable, intra-specific competition and aggression have become predominant. We have an evolutionary impasse.

The ethologist's position has been expounded in relative detail because he thinks in terms of man long before the Sermon on the Mount. The book is full of extrapolations from animal behaviour to human behaviour. We have already referred to the relations between love and hate. Elsewhere, Lorenz implies that the phylogenetic species ritual is repeated in the cultural ritual of mankind. In both cases, 'what appears to us, on superficial examination, as one ceremony, often consists of a whole number of behavioural elements eliciting each other mutually' (ibid, p. 55). Cultural ritual has the same three-fold function as ritual transmitted by heredity. 'This again is important for our theme, because it is particularly the drives that have arisen by ritualization which are so often called upon, in this parliament, to oppose aggression, to divert it into harmless channels, and to inhibit those of its actions that are injurious to the survival of the species' (ibid, p. 56). This is followed by an illustration of the omnipresence of ritual in social behaviour. It ensures the cohesion of groups which are too big to be bound together by interpersonal ties, and the survival of cultural species.

There is a similar basis for the other restraint on aggressiveness, the inter-individual relationship.

It is an observation familiar to anybody who has travelled in trains that well-bred people behave atrociously towards strangers in the territorial defence of their compartment. When they discover that the intruder is an acquaintance, however casual, there is an amazing and ridiculous switch in their behaviour from extreme rudeness to exaggerated and shamefaced politeness (ibid, p. 244).

Other comparisons are referred to in less detail, such as those relating to the dissociation between physical love and romantic love, to hospitality, to feelings or to the attachment to one's home.

The passage concerned with the 'roll-cackle' characteristic of the assembling of the great migratory flocks is more directly relevant to the study of intergroup behaviour. Within these flocks, the members of the goose family close ranks and chase away the members of other breeds. On the basis of this behaviour, Lorenz extrapolates thus:

Discriminative aggression towards strangers and the bond between the members of a group enhance each other. The opposition of 'we' and 'they' can unite some widely contrasting units. Confronted with present-day China, the United States and the Soviet Union occasionally seem to feel as 'we'. The same phenomenon, which incidentally has some of the earmarks of war, can be studied in the roll-cackle ceremony of greylag geese (ibid, p. 162).

According to Lorenz, these comparisons are not just analogies. We have no hesitation in using the same term 'eye' with respect to certain cephalopoda and to vertebrates. 'We are equally justified in omitting the inverted commas when speaking of the social behaviour patterns of higher animals which are analogous with those of man' (ibid, p. 188). However, 'None of our western languages has an intransitive verb to do justice to the increase of values produced by nearly every step in evolution. One cannot possibly call it development when something new and higher arises from an earlier stage which does not contain the constituent properties for the new and higher being' (ibid, p. 195).

The two-fold assertion of similarity or identity and of superiority does not really clarify the precise nature of the comparisons which the ethologist makes. His work suffers from a major defect – in the comparison which is made, one of the two sides has been subject to careful research, the other has not been studied at all. His analyses of animal behaviour brought the author the Nobel prize; there has been virtually no investigation of the complex technical and symbolic devices in terms of which man has developed his 'history of nature' (Moscovici, 1968). Lorenz, like a conjurer, produces startling results, leaving much concealed. Light is cast upon only one aspect of the situation. The similarity in isolated behavioural structures is remarkable and may well indicate a common origin. But there is no justification for assuming that these structures, once they are integrated into new structures, may not assume fresh significance and obey new functional laws. The example of the eye is relevant here. No-one denies the similarity between the eye of the cuttle-fish and the human eye, but this does not mean that what each eye sees is identical. Developmental research on size constancy shows that, even in man, perception changes when more advanced cognitive operations are involved. We have here an example of a structure which is integrated into a further, higher order structure. It might be thought that this is what Lorenz means when he says that the inferior does not explain the superior. But he does not respect the implications of his own position when, for example, he writes, 'The principle of the bond, formed by having something in common which has to be defended against outsiders, remains the same, from cichlids defending a common territory or brood, right up to scientists defending a common opinion and – most dangerous of all – the fanatics defending a common ideology. In all these cases aggression is necessary to enhance the bond'

(Lorenz, 1969, p. 163). Is the function of ideology in a social system really the same thing as the significance of territory for animals?

It is a mistake to attribute the same effects to the same causes without qualification. There may well be a connection between aggression and social cohesion in animals and men; but we must still specify the relevant dynamic process in both cases. For example, how do scientists or 'fanatics' defend their theory or their ideology and why do they attack a different position? As long as behaviours of this kind have not been studied in their proper context it is premature to assert that there is the same connection between aggression and cohesiveness in different species.

There are other examples of facile comparisons. Some are based on no more than anecdotes. Lorenz's aunt never kept a servant longer than eight or ten months. This anecdote was advanced as a manifestation of the aggressive instinct in man. But many other factors, both economic and social, might have induced a middle-class Austrian lady to change her servant at regular intervals. Lorenz equates the rigidity with which the law is respected with the rigidity with which animals perform their phylogenetic rituals. But surely it is also the case that the law is inculcated by certain social groups, precisely because this law reflects a balance of forces which is in their favour. The latter explanation has at least the advantage of indicating why different groups within a single social structure do not respect the law with an equal degree of rigidity.

According to Lorenz, neuro-physiological manifestations phylogenetically inherited accompany militant enthusiasm.

In reality, militant enthusiasm is a specialized form of communal aggression, clearly distinct from and yet functionally related to the more primitive forms of petty individual aggression. Every man of normally strong emotions knows, from his own experience, the subjective phenomena that go hand in hand with the response of militant enthusiasm. A shiver runs down the back, and, as more exact observation shows, along the outside of both arms. One soars elated above all the ties of everyday life (ibid, p. 231).

Unfortunately, this account tells us nothing about the specific dynamic properties of ideological movements, artistic trends or scientific debates. At best, it tells us that the reactions transmitted phylogenetically have been reorganised into new systems, the particular rules relating to which are of a symbolic and social nature, and not the subject of study by the ethologist.

We still have to explain the development of those inheritances from the past when they are integrated into more recent structures. Piaget has touched upon the problem; although his special interest has been in cognitive structures in man, he does not hesitate to speak of the 'bursting of instinct' (1971, p. 366). According to Piaget, in man, hereditary programming may give way to new forms of self-regulation of a cognitive nature.

COGNITIVE DETERMINANTS OF AGGRESSIVENESS

The importance of cognitive factors in the control of aggression has been investigated by Berkowitz. His studies provide a useful complement to Lorenz's book, although their scope is much less ambitious.

In a short article, Berkowitz (1965) justifies experimental studies of aggression. The frustration–aggression hypothesis lies behind most of his work. Frustration is represented by any obstacle to satisfaction encountered by goal-directed behaviour, and it creates tension within the organism which is discharged by aggressive behaviour. Thus, frustration leads to aggression. But is this relationship an inborn one? Some claim that it is. Berkowitz (1965), however, does not think it necessary to posit innateness. He also finds the hypothesis relating aggression to frustration inadequate on its own; factors other than frustration, for example imitation, may be sufficient to release aggression (Bandura and Walters, 1963). And every frustration does not necessarily lead to aggression; it may sometimes lead simply to an intensification of reactions which are then interpreted by the observer as aggressive acts, although the individual has no intention of hurting anybody. Berkowitz's position, then, is that frustration only creates a certain 'readiness' for aggression and that other specific kinds of stimulation are necessary to provoke aggressive behaviour. The probability of occurrence and the strength of aggressive acts are thus, according to Berkowitz, a function of two factors – the nature of the releasers which in certain cases can provoke aggression in the absence of any kind of frustration, and the strength of the readiness for aggression produced by frustration. Although instinct may still be involved, account must also be taken of the particular nature of the releasers, which may be symbolic in nature. Berkowitz's experiments are specifically directed toward the investigation of such releasers. We shall summarise one of these experiments (Geen and Berkowitz, 1966).

Ninety subjects took part in the experiment, which was designed to study some of the conditions under which a film of a scene of violence may provoke aggressive behaviour in the viewer. Half of the subjects watched first a film in which a character called Dunne violently assaulted his rival Midge Kelly. The other half of the subjects watched a film of a race in which two first-class runners competed against one another for victory and broke a record. Having watched these films, the subjects were asked to participate in a learning task. Every subject took part along with another person who was in fact an experimenter's accomplice. The naive subject had to punish the accomplice's mistakes by giving him mild electric shocks.

For one third of the subjects in each case, the other person was said to be called Bob Kelly, Bob Dunne or Bob Riley. The independent variables in the experiment were therefore the presence or absence of a scene of violence before the learning task, and the presence or absence of homonymy between the victim in the filmed scene (Midge Kelly) and the potential victim in the learning session (Bob Kelly). Further, for another third of the subjects, one of the potential victims also had an Irish name (Bob Riley) and thus represented, like the protagonist Kelly, a minority group often the object of aggression (the experiment was carried out in the United States). In this experiment, the authors were trying to verify the hypothesis, previously partly supported by the experiments of Berkowitz (1965) and Berkowitz and Geen (1966), that presenting a scene of violence intensifies aggressive reactions especially when the viewers are confronted with a potential victim who is associated in some way with the victim in the scene presented. The hypothesis was indeed supported, as is indicated by Table 1. It should also be noted that the fact that a person belongs to the same group as the victim tends to increase the degree of aggression directed against him.

Table 1. *Mean number of shocks delivered to accomplice*

Accomplice's name	Boxing film	Track film
Kelly	5.40	3.60
Dunne	4.15	3.87
Riley	4.40	4.00

SOURCE: Geen and Berkowitz, 1966.

More complex mechanisms than those studied by Berkowitz are undoubtedly involved in the release of aggressive behaviour. His experiment does, however, show that cognitive factors are involved in the processes leading to aggression. These cognitive factors derive from the social context and concern interpersonal relationships which essentially can be accommodated within the category differentiation model, which will be described in Part II, Chapter 2.

FREUD AS SOCIAL PSYCHOLOGIST

It has always been tempting to use psychoanalytic theory to explain the conflicts and tensions involved in a social structure. Although the analogy between structural conflict at the individual level and structural conflict at the social

level may provide a working hypothesis, this does not necessarily mean that merely arguing from one level to the other
will do much to advance our understanding. The reference
to the work of Lorenz has already shown the dangers implicit
in any such procedure. Freud (1955), contrary to many of
his followers, seemed to be aware of the problem when
he dealt with the relations between individual and group
psychology, in a book written in a period of transition
between his earlier conception of ego function and his later
conception.

The aim of *Group Psychology and the Analysis of the Ego*
is said to be as follows:

If a Psychology, concerned with exploring the predispositions, the
instincts, the motives and the aims of an individual man down to
his actions and his relations with those who are nearest to him, had
completely achieved its task, and had cleared up the whole of
these matters and their interconnections, it would then suddenly
find itself confronted by a new task which would lie before it
unachieved. It would be obliged to explain the surprising fact that
under a certain condition this individual whom it had come to
understand thought, felt and acted in quite a different way from
what would have been expected. And this condition is his insertion
into a collection of people which has acquired the characteristic
of a 'psychological group'. What, then, is a 'group'? (Freud, 1955,
p. 72).

To answer this question, Freud begins by summarising
the description of the crowd given by Le Bon in 1895.
According to Le Bon, the heterogeneity of the individuals
disappears and is replaced by homogeneity due to hereditary
influences and ancestral residues which make up the racial
mind. A feeling of power takes possession of crowds and
lowers their responsibility; the members of a crowd are
bound together by genuine mental contagion. Freud wondered whether the cause of this contagion might not be the
same as that underlying hypnosis. Crowd behaviour is
characterised by spontaneity, violence, heroism and extremity. This collection of new characteristics is regarded as
justifying the expression 'collective mind'. Freud goes on

to compare the crowd as described by Le Bon with the individual child, the neurotic and the primitive.

Before continuing our discussion of Freud, we should like to point out that the description of the crowd which he took from Le Bon has not been completely abandoned. The work on risk-taking in groups (Kogan and Wallach, 1967), to which we shall refer again later, from the beginning involved reference to the dilution of responsibility which the group tends to produce, as an explanatory factor. Again, Zimbardo (1969) has shown that conditions of anonymity favour the appearance of violent behaviour. A number of experiments also indicate that situations which call for group decisions or group judgments tend to lead to the adoption of extreme positions (Doise, 1969c).

However, other descriptions of groups were available to Freud when he was writing his book. McDougall's (1920) account was of particular interest to psychoanalysts because it was concerned with organised groups. Groups of this kind are characterised by greater continuity, by an idea which mobilises the feelings of members of the group, by rivalry with other groups, by norms concerning relations between members, and by the presence of organisation leading to specialisation and differentiation of labour. These are issues which have since been of major concern to the experimental study of group dynamics. Freud takes up McDougall's account and contends that organised groups succeed in re-creating individual qualities. The exaggerated emotionality and the drop in intelligence which Le Bon describes may thus be counterbalanced by organisation.

There is therefore no contradiction between Le Bon and McDougall. Both, like Tarde, appeal to suggestion as an explanatory principle. Freud had already found this notion in Bernheim and taken exception to it. 'Later on my resistance took the direction of protesting against the view that suggestion, which explained everything, was itself to be preserved from explanation' (Freud, 1955, p. 89).

The explanations of suggestion and its application to collective psychology are developed in the rest of the book.

Libidinal attachment lies behind suggestion. It is in organised groups, like the army and the church, that this attachment is most clearly expressed. It takes two forms, attachment to the leader and attachment to the other members. Libidinal ties, as in other contexts, are more significant than purely practical advantages, and do not have a directly sexual aim. The process of identification by which a person takes over a characteristic, a point of view or an attribute of another person, illustrates this point of view. The Ego is enriched by introjection of Other. Another form of attachment can be seen in the ties involved in love and in hypnosis, where the ego-criticising function or ego-ideal, is replaced by the love-object or by the hypnotist. In groups like the church and the army, the members all replace their ego-ideal by the same object, Christ or the leader. Again, when they are all treated equally by their leaders, they very quickly give up their jealousy, recognise their mutuality, and identify with one another. Modern crowds are thus essentially like the primitive horde, except that, in the case of the primitive horde, the chief regarded his followers with hatred, while in the army and the church, according to Freud, Love is the crucial factor.

We shall end this account of Freud by referring to his comparative account of different forms of libidinal attachment.

Being in love is based upon the simultaneous presence of directly sexual tendencies and of sexual tendencies that are inhibited in their aims, so that the object draws a part of the narcissistic ego-libido to itself. It is a condition in which there is only room for the ego and the object.

Hypnosis resembles being in love in being limited to these two persons, but it is based entirely upon sexual tendencies that are inhibited in their aims and substitutes the object for the ego ideal.

The group multiplies this process; it agrees with hypnosis in the nature of the instincts which hold it together, and in the replacement of the ego ideal by the object; but to this it adds identification with other individuals, which was perhaps originally made possible by their having the same relation to the object (Freud, 1955, pp. 142–3).

Freud therefore proposes a synchronic explanation of society. He describes the processes by which individuals are able to become part of a social unit. The effect of the sharing of a common fate has also been investigated experimentally by Rabbie and Horwitz (1969), whose study will be outlined later.

Freud also raises the question of how certain persons become the ego-ideal of others. According to him, this amounts to asking how, in his 'just so story' of the primitive horde, some members of the horde were able to become individuals and 'one of a number' of fathers of families. The myth itself may have been important in the process, enabling the individual to emerge from the crowd by identifying himself with the hero who defeated the chief. This hero himself is the personification of a common act. Individual development also depends upon the satisfaction of the individual's direct sexual impulses and their fixation upon a woman. The role of representation in the integration of individual and group was therefore recognised by Freud. We shall return to this question later.

Occasionally Freud mentions intergroup relations, remarking, for example, that the weakening of attachments within the group should be associated with greater tolerance with respect to the members of other groups. The study of intergroup and intra-group attachments is a constant object of attention in research on intergroup relations. If a causal mechanism is involved, it does not act only in the way described by Freud. Experimentally, the influence of intergroup relations upon relations within the group is more securely established than vice versa.

The existence of a measure of aggressiveness between similar groups calls for some kind of explanation.

Of two neighbouring towns each is the other's most jealous rival; every little canton looks down upon the others with contempt. Closely related races keep one another at arm's length; the South German cannot endure the North German . . . In the undisguised antipathies and aversions which people feel towards strangers with whom they have to do we may recognize the expression of self-love

– of narcissism. This self-love works ior the self-assertion of the individual, and behaves as though the occurrence of any divergence from his own particular lines of development involved a criticism of them and a demand for their alteration. We do not know why such sensitiveness should have been directed to just these details of differentiation; but it is unmistakable that in this whole connection men give evidence of a readiness for hatred, an aggressiveness, the source of which is unknown, and to which one is tempted to ascribe an elementary character (Freud, 1955, pp. 101–2).

Only in a footnote is an interpretation given in terms of instinct, 'In a recently published study ["Beyond the Pleasure Principle", Freud, 1955, pp. 7–64], I have attempted to connect the polarity of love and hatred with a hypothetical opposition between instincts of life and death, and to establish the sexual instincts as the purest examples of the former, the instincts of life' (Freud, 1955, p. 102). Let us consider for a moment the difference between this 'instinctual' interpretation, which avoids analysis of details, and the much more detailed explanations of 'organised groups' in terms of identification and ego ideal.

   Explanation in terms of such libidinal attachments is limited. Freud himself (ibid, p. 94) admits that,

An objection will justly be raised against this conception of the libidinal structure of an army on the ground that no place has been found in it for such ideas as those of one's country, of national glory, etc., which are of such importance in holding an army together. The answer is that that is a different instance of a group tie, and no longer such a simple one; for the examples of great generals, like Caesar, Wallenstein, or Napoleon, show that such ideas are not indispensable to the existence of an army.

Although notions of one's native land and of national glory are not regarded as essential, they are nevertheless recognised as factors belonging to 'a quite different order'. They should therefore be studied at their own level, especially since we assume that identification with the 'great leaders' is possible through the mediation of ideas. It may also be noted that Freud offers no analysis of the role of coercive power in the army.

PSYCHOGENESIS OF INTERGROUP RELATIONS

Piaget's theory is particularly impressive in its coherence and scope. It is relevant to the psychological development of cognitive operations and to the way in which the individual interprets the cognitive rules which govern his interaction with the environment. The idea of one's native land and of relations with other countries is one of the cognitive instruments which the individual in our society has to acquire in the course of his development. How is he able to do so?

In the course of studies aimed at answering this question, Piaget and Weil were struck by a paradox.

This paradox is as follows. Far from being primary data, or even occurring early in development, the sentiment and even the very notion of one's native land appear only relatively late in the normal child, and there seems to be nothing implying an inevitable development toward patriotic sociocentrism. On the contrary, to reach an intellectual and effective awareness of his own country, the child has to decentre (with respect to his town, his district etc.) and to co-ordinate (with perspectives other than his own) – processes which enable him to approach an understanding of countries and points of view other than his own (Piaget and Weil, 1951, p. 605).

We shall proceed to give an account of this process of decentration and co-ordination, a process which appears to work against the commonly observed patriotic sociocentrism.

The children questioned were pupils of Geneva schools; the responses did not differ essentially between Swiss children and foreign children. The authors describe first how the idea of one's native land develops, from an intellectual point of view. Up to seven or eight years of age, children may say that their town is in Switzerland, but are unable to see that Geneva is part of a whole. When they are asked to draw Geneva and Switzerland, they draw two juxtaposed circles. It is only during the next stage of intellectual development (from 7 or 8 to 10 or 11 years of age) that the inclusion of their town in Switzerland is understood. During this period, however, they do not yet master the logical inclusion of classes. One cannot be both a Swiss and a Genevan. For children at this stage, Genevans are often non-Swiss. Accurate systematisation of these notions is not achieved until later. And how about the affective side? This aspect was studied by asking the child to express his preferences for the different countries he knew of. The responses correspond to the stages of cognitive development. The very young child does not express any systematic preference for his native land. Preferences are based on immediate and transitory personal interests, such as, '. . . I like Italy, they have very good cakes, not like Switzerland where things are enough to make you cry. . .' (ibid, p. 609). At the second stage, Switzerland begins to be preferred with a kind of family devotion – because one is born there, because it is the country of one's father and mother, because it is one's own country. Justifications of one's affective attachment to one's country change during the third stage, and find expression through collective notions like liberty, neutrality, the country spared by the war, the Red Cross. The child of this age knows that there is a wider society with its own values, other than his own, than that of his family and of his town, and other than the visible and concrete realities with which he is surrounded.

The responses of the children with respect to other nations show the same logical and affective structure. At the first stage, the child finds it equally difficult to include his own country in a greater whole. His value judgments are based on subjective and short-lasting motives. In the second stage, the child gives up his subjective and short-lasting judgments, and takes over from his family or from his immediate environment, judgments favourable or/unfavourable to other countries. The discovery of a more widely extended whole is possible only in the third stage, in which there may be understanding of differences along with some degree of relativity.

The notion of 'foreigner' enables us to study the intellectual aspect of reciprocity. For the youngest subjects, foreigners are clearly always 'the others'. They cannot have become foreigners, even by going to live in another country. The child at the intermediate stage is not so sure about it, and at the third stage, the intellectual concept of 'foreigners' has definitely been attained. From the cognitive point of view, there is no longer any obstacle to the understanding of reciprocal relationships. It may be asked whether there are corresponding obstacles at the affective level. The child was again asked about his preferences, but this time his attention was drawn to his native country and he was asked what the answer of children of other countries would be. At the first stage the child chose his own country, and according to him, children of other countries would also choose Switzerland: '. . . because it's better in Switzerland . . ., because they know the Swiss are nicer . . .' (ibid, p. 619). The attribution of a corresponding choice to children of other countries becomes possible only during the second stage. Even so, at this stage, the child who is questioned does not resist the counter-suggestion in the question, 'Who is right?' He is right and not the foreigner who chooses his own country. Reciprocity in respect of this aspect is also acquired during the third stage.

Nevertheless, despite this capacity for affective and cognitive reciprocity, we still find the signs of nationalist sociocentrism in adults. Piaget in fact describes cognitive development as a succession of centrations and decentrations. The child first of all centres on transitory interests and points of view. He then frees himself from those and is able to share in common interests and points of view, such as those of his family or his native town. Finally, he becomes capable of mastering the widest point of view, transcending that of his own and other countries. How then can we account for the patriotic sociocentrism which we find so often among adults?

To explain the ready appearance later of the various forms of nationalist sociocentrism, we must either accept the sudden appearance of influences other than those appearing during the child's previous development (and it is by no means clear how such influences might become effective), or we must accept the fact that the very same factors which acted against the initial decentrations and co-ordinations (from the formation of the notion of native country) reappear at all levels and form the most general cause of the deviations and tensions. Our own interpretation tends to favour the second alternative (ibid, pp. 605–6).

This is clarified by Piaget's pronouncements elsewhere. Inhelder and Piaget (1958), in a book devoted to the development of logic in child and adolescent, give a more detailed account of the interplay of centration and decentration, in terms of which intellectual operations develop. They describe centrations as the result of disequilibration between the processes of assimilation, which integrate new objects into transposable and generalisable schemata of action, and the processes of accommodation, which mediate the application of the same schemata to the outside world. An imaginary assimilation of the environment to the ego may prevail over the adaptation of the ego to the environment. This can still happen when the adolescent masters the logic of hypothetico-deductive and abstract proof.

. . . the adolescent goes through a phase in which he attributes an unlimited power to his own thoughts so that the dream of a glorious future or of transforming the world through ideas. . . seems to be not only fantasy but also an effective action which in itself modifies the empirical world. This is obviously a form of cognitive egocentrism. Although it differs sharply from the child's egocentrism. . . it results, nevertheless, from the same mechanism and appears as a function of the new conditions created by the structuring of formal thought (Inhelder and Piaget, 1958, pp. 345–6).

Nationalistic sociocentrism would thus represent one form of centration of abstract thought. But although it may be regarded in this way at the individual level, it must also be regarded in terms of on-going social processes with which Piaget, as a psychologist, was not concerned. We must therefore study sociocentrism not only as an expression of individual thought, but also as '. . . a system of relations each of which, as a relation, implies a transformation of the terms which it relates' (Piaget, 1965, p. 29).

With the exception of commonsense psychology, approaches so far have been characterised by an attempt to be consistent in their explanation of individual behaviour, in each case a more or less thoroughly developed conceptual framework being used to give more general significance to aggression, to mankind's capacity for association and to the cognitive and affective development of human modes of participation in wider social units. The main aim of these attempts has not been to study the possible variations among different individuals in the way in which they take part in certain modes of social relations, but to clarify the more general mechanisms which enable an individual to take part in a given network of social relations.

Clinical psychologists have a different aim; their work is primarily concerned not with general aspects but with what is characteristic of a particular individual case. Studies of this kind are, of course, only possible in so far as general ideas have been developed about the ways in which people can be differentiated. Ideas of this kind, on which personality tests are based, do not necessarily have very general explanatory value. They define parameters with a view to placing certain individuals in relation to others at a given moment in their life.

In respect to our own field of interest, Smith, Bruner and White (1956), within the more general context of a study of the relations between personality and opinion, adopt a similar clinical approach. The purpose of their investigation was to see how different personalities, defined in terms of several parameters, developed political opinions and attitudes. The study was carried out in the United States in 1947. The subjects were American citizens, and the investigators studied their opinions about and attitudes toward the Soviet Union.

Each subject took part in 15 sessions of about two hours each. They all took intelligence tests and personality tests, and answered questionnaires dealing with their knowledge of the Soviet Union. Several interviews were devoted to investigating their opinions in general, and their opinions concerning the Soviet Union. Contradictions which appeared in what was said by each subject were also discussed. We shall give here only the main conclusions which the authors reached.

Opinions concerning the Soviet Union first of all appeared to be an expression of the personalities of the individuals expressing them, i.e. of their intelligence, of their general mood and of the dynamic quality shown in the various tests and other experimental situations. The authors then describe opinions as having three functions, evaluation of the social environment, adjustment to the groups constituting this environment and finally, the resolution of personal problems.

First, let us consider some examples of what the authors mean by the expressive nature of opinions. An individual's opinions express his personality in so far as they reflect relations between abstract and concrete intelligence and between reflection and affect. Thus, among the subjects of the study, it is the most intellectually gifted who presents more arguments for and against, has the most differentiated picture of the Soviet Union and who gives most consideration to the view that the Russian political system represents an ideology defending a system of values.

One's opinions reflect the general direction of one's mood; there is the attitude of resignation of the person who no longer has any personal ambition and puts all his hopes on the future of an ideology (sic), the pessimism of another who sees evil everywhere and especially in the development of Soviet power, and the optimism of a third who believes that competition between the United States and the Soviet Union will lead to a third kind of society which will transcend the existing hostility between the two Powers. The dynamics of his own personality lead another subject to express opinions mainly concerned with the immediate measures his country should take, while a more passive subject thinks that it is essential above all things not to offend a great power seeking world domination. Opinions express personality traits in the same way as projective tests.

To illustrate the principal two functions of opinion, we shall examine, for each, the most important three cases studied by the authors. How do opinions work in their role in evaluating the environment?

After studying law, Chatwell was successful in his profession as a barrister. The existing economic system gave him a number of advantages, and he believed in a free world allowing the individual to develop his talents, to realise his potential and to succeed in his profession in a social framework protected by laws. His attitude to the Soviet Union fits into this whole; 'he espoused her right to develop her productive economy in her own way, free from outside interference, but he deplored the police state, the suppression of individual initiative, and the forceful, illegal methods of dealing with neighbour countries' (Smith, Bruner and White, 1956, p. 110).

Lanlin, who was the father of four children, had failed in an administrative capacity and, at the time of the study, was a sales representative in the same company. He was satisfied with his current job and with the opportunities for promotion which it offered. What was important for him was to attain economic security by accumulating property. What was his attitude to the Soviet Union? He saw it as a country ruled by a group of people who showed plenty of assurance but who were actually dependent upon the Americans. He identified with the United States, the social system upon which he and, according to him, the Soviet Union, were both dependent.

Sullivan had not made a success of his life and gave up all hope of doing so. After thirty years, his failures led to a period of alcoholism. Following this, a job with the press put him in touch with a group of Communists. The Soviet Union embodied his sole hope of progress toward a just world. 'The Russia that he saw, the embodiment of all that was new and hopeful, was furthering his values of justice, progress and social welfare' (ibid, p. 187).

There we have the evaluative function of the three individuals' opinions. Let us now illustrate the social group membership function which these same opinions also serve.

Chatwell, a privileged member of the system, takes his place in it by competition and discussion, identifying himself with the ideal of the free and rational man. Just as competition characterises his own relations with his immediate environment, it may also, according to him, characterise the business of relations between countries.

Lanlin conforms to the environment on which he depends. He identifies with the management of his firm. 'In this sense, then, Lanlin's opinions served both in his social adjustment by concretizing his allegiance to the society with which he identified . . . For the condemnation of Russia as the unruly, demanding, aggressive, unreasonable nation was an affirmation of his own early and continuing renunciation of "making demands that didn't make sense"' (ibid, p. 152).

Sullivan directs his need for social recognition to a small group of friends. When the opportunity arises, he likes to provoke, shock and draw attention to himself. He identifies with a far-off group of revolutionary intellectuals. Nonconformity for him represents a strategy by which to assert his different point of view and, therefore, to feel superior when he shocks others.

There is finally the function of externalisation of opinions, which is more difficult to detect. The authors speak of externalisation when a person reacts to an external event in a way which is influenced by his unresolved personal problems. This would be the case when unconscious impulses influence the perception of social objects. Thus, a person with an inferiority complex would be externalising it if he regarded the Russians as under the power of a small group of potentially dangerous rulers. Attitudes to his own impulses would equally influence his social attitudes. The father of a family with a tendency to be aggressive toward his own family would condemn the tolerance of the Russians in the matter of divorce. The strategies which have brought personal success tend to be extrapolated to the social field. The individual who succeeds by taking a strong line tends to advocate a hard attitude toward the Soviet Union. The authors do, however, remark that the presence of the function of externalisation varies greatly between individuals and that, in some people, projective tests reveal a much more fragile picture than that indicated by studying their opinions in depth. It would seem likely that this may be because the test situation, in a way, removes the subject from the influence of his dominant social attachments, while normally individuals are able to manage things in such a way as not to threaten their role in a given social system.

The conclusion to be drawn from the account of the expressive nature and the function of opinions given by Smith, Bruner and White would seem to be that they occupy a borderline position between personality structure and social structure. Their place within the personality structure certainly influences the nature of the characteristics which are reflected in an individual's opinions; but it is doubtful whether these personality characteristics can sensibly be studied without account being taken of the significance of the 'sociological' function which opinions about the Soviet Union served for American society at the beginning of the cold war. The authors show no interest in this question. Under the significant heading 'informational environment', a mere seven or eight pages are devoted to the historical context of the period; beyond this, opinions are treated as data which each individual assimilates in his own way, as a function of his individual history, and no explanation of them in social terms is given. Social functions of evaluation and group membership clearly cannot be studied at the individual level alone. Consider the case of Chatwell; by profession, he is used to handling arguments. Accordingly, he favours a rational approach to relations with the Soviet Union, which should be developed in the United Nations. Surely the professional activity which involves him in manipulating arguments and counter-arguments represents *par excellence* the result of an ideological position which favours a negotiated solution to conflicts between parties. What then is the role of such an ideology? How is it connected with the opinions, ideas and attitudes which American society was led to produce for or against the Communist Soviet Union? Smith, Bruner and White have studied only one aspect of a total process. The 'personality characteristics', as they call them, are a function of the position occupied by their subjects in a social structure to at least as great an extent as they themselves influence certain aspects of the representations of this social position.

It is thus scarcely surprising that this failure to distinguish between levels of explanation leads the authors of *Opinions and Personality* to rather tautological explanations. It is surely not remarkable, for example, that individuals capable of expressing themselves intelligently in the range of situations covered by the tests, should also express themselves intelligently when they are asked about their political opinions. A more important question would be, under what conditions these people *failed* to express themselves intelligently. Generally speaking, the explanation of opinions in terms of personality takes no account of their content; this is another limitation which the authors' approach imposes. Surely the content of opinions should also be taken into consideration, when their functional aspect is described. It may often be wondered how far the explanation given might not serve equally well to cast light upon quite different reactions. Consider the example of a person who finds it difficult to succeed in American society, closes his eyes to any other alternative and expresses in an undifferentiated way his hostility to the Soviet Union. Such an individual might well react like Sullivan and put his hopes in the Soviet Union. Both reactions are equally comprehensible.

An approach at the individual level, with personality tests, may in some conditions predict the content of political opinions and attitudes. By taking account of the social position of our subjects, we ourselves were able to confirm the existence of a relation between personality and political opinions (Doise, 1969b). It is reasonable to think that the way in which an individual takes part in a system of social relations is partly determined by his previous social experience. Using the Authoritarianism scale (F-scale), Adorno, Frenkel-Brunswick, Levinson and Sanford (1950) developed an instrument for measuring submissiveness to the established order and existing institutions of a given social system, while Rokeach (1960) has provided us with a Dogmatism scale measuring the relatively uncritical acceptance of belief-systems current in the individual's society.

These two conceptions of personality factors are clearly not yet a sufficient basis for predicting the opinions and attitudes with regard to international politics, of subjects showing the syndromes of authoritarianism or dogmatism. Further proof of this was given by a pre-enquiry in which we interviewed subjects with very different political and social affiliations. In our attempt to establish a relation between personality factors and political opinions, we had to study subjects whose social position was clearly defined. Our subjects were male pupils in the top classes of Catholic colleges in what were then the Common Market countries (with the exception of Luxemburg). In the years 1965–6, the majority of these pupils, as our questionnaire confirmed, shared the ideas of the socio-political groups who were then in power in their country. Thus, for these subjects, it was possible to make predictions about the relations between authoritarianism and dogmatism on the one hand, and the way in which they shared the representations and attitudes produced by their environment in the field of international relations, on the other hand.

The main predictions to be verified as regards the authoritarian syndrome were as follows. Authoritarians are especially likely to establish distance between themselves or their compatriots and foreigners who are already held at a distance by their national group; they accentuate differences between countries, more frequently adhering to the political institutions of their own country and to the international policy of the super power of the Western alliance, which they are also more willing to admit to an economic and political Union with the Six; they allow for little international reciprocity, are more nationalistic both in the narrow sense and in the wider European sense, and in consequence, reject open Europeanism and even European supranationality in any sense. This complex of relations may be described as representing adherence to an established state of affairs – keep well separated what is separate, be favourable to and even ally oneself with the strong power which defends at the international level the currently existing state of affairs, and resist any change at the European level except where such a change represents a reinforcing of the established order, for example, through European nationalism.

Dogmatism is associated with an absence of perceived understanding between North Americans and Russians, with an absence of understanding between our subjects and the Russians and with a preference for the political institutions of their country and rejection of the Soviet Union's international policy. Dogmatism also goes with more frequent willingness to admit the United States to an Economic Union with the Six, but not with acceptance of international reciprocity. It is more frequently associated with nationalism, European nationalism and even European supranationalism, and with a tendency to see European unification as near to realisation. It seems to us that the effective common denominator of all these relations is the more or less exclusive adherence to one cause and the incapacity to reconcile several points of view on international affairs.

On the basis of certain personality traits, which are themselves the result of a whole complex of social interactions, it is thus possible to make predictions about the content of the perceptions and attitudes of certain individuals within a given social system, provided that account is taken of the particular social position of the subjects in this system.

These results should not, however, make us forget that the approach to international relations is determined first

and foremost by factors other than personality characteristics. In the research referred to we took care to control for
the socio-economic factor, and, in the case of some questions, nationality, so that the influence of personality factors
might be made clear. Later, we became more interested in
studying the role of representations and attitudes in the
specific dynamics of intergroup relations. The very changes
in these relations are probably important causes in the
appearance of authoritarian and dogmatic behaviour in the
members of the interacting groups.

Other 'psychologies' directly or indirectly relevant to the
object of our study might have been discussed. Doubtless
they also would imply some kind of sociological approach.
Our thesis, in fact, is that a purely psychological study of
intergroup relations is impossible. At the psychological
level, we can at most describe mechanisms which allow the
individual to engage in new interactions, but which
themselves develop in social interaction. These new interactions have their own particular characteristics, especially
when they take place between groups or between individuals
who belong to different categories or groups.

2

The sociological approach

This chapter is not intended to give an account of different 'sociologies' of significance for the study of intergroup relations. That is the business of professional sociologists. Our task is to assess the relevance of certain ideas developed at the sociological level, to the possibility of an integration of psychology and sociology in the field. These ideas are to be found mainly in the body of thinking which has emerged around the concept of ideology. Ideology plays an important part in the development of intergroup relations. Moreover, it is in the study of ideologies that the problems of the limits of sociological explanation in particular and scientific explanation in general arise most acutely.

The line we shall take means that we must first of all review briefly the Marxist conception of the role played by ideology in a social system. We shall then show how more complex approaches complement this. And finally, we shall describe some of the typical ways in which ideology functions, and end our excursion into sociology with a discussion of the links between scientific and ideological activity.

IDEOLOGIES AND SOCIAL SYSTEMS

A social system is characterised by its particular relations of production. Thus, capitalist society represents a system in which the forces of production are not the owners of the means of production, which allows the owners of these means of production to deprive the producers of part of the product of their work. The forces of production, however,

33

develop scientifically and technically, which emphasises their antagonism toward those who possess the means of production. The Marxist conception of ideology developed within this basic framework.

Althusser gives the following definition of ideology.

It will suffice to know very schematically that an ideology is a system (with its own logic and rigour) of representations (images, myths, ideas or concepts, depending on the case) endowed with a historical existence and role within a given society. Without embarking on the problem of the relations between a science and its (ideological) past, we may say that ideology, as a system of representations, is distinguished from science in that in it the practico-social function is more important than the theoretical function (function as knowledge) (Althusser, 1969, p. 231).

We shall discuss later the distinction made here between ideology and science. For the moment, we shall try to explain what is meant by the existence and historical function of ideology.

A distinction must be made between dominant and op- posing ideologies. The function of the former is to ensure the reproduction and reinforcement of the existing system of productive relations. To this end, the dominant ideology has at its disposal the various ideological apparatuses of the State, such as schools, churches and legal system. These institutions mediate and in some measure elaborate the dominant ideology, in terms of which they justify the exist- ing mode of production and social order. This ideology claims justification in terms of natural and universal truths. What is characteristic of a particular status in a given social system becomes interpreted as an expression of human nature. There then emerges, in opposition to this dominant ideology, an ideology of the dominated or proletarian classes. The function of this ideology is to enable members of these classes to become aware of their exploited position and of the fact that a change in the relations of production would make them masters of the whole product of their labour. In this sense, the opposing ideology is more true to life, because it makes clear the contradictions which the dominant ideology conceals.

This description of the social status of ideology is, of course, only a brief one, and reflects no more than the core of current Marxist thinking; it might conceivably give rise to a mechanistic interpretation of ideology, which is something we are anxious to avoid. As Althusser reminds us in his definition, we are concerned with a system which has its own logic and necessity. The determining influence which the relations of production (infrastructure) exercise upon ideology (superstructure) does not represent a case of one-way causality; the ideological aspect exercises a reciprocal influence on the infrastructure. Thus, by various intervening steps, the apparatuses of the dominant ideology serve to reinforce the existing relations of production. This explains the importance attached to the ideological struggle by those who appeal to historical materialism. A second reason for rejecting the notion of blind materialism lies in just that ideological autonomy to which Althusser refers. Although it may be agreed that the development of social relations contributes to the development of ideology, and in a way powers this development, Marxist authors nevertheless hold that this development is governed by its own laws. An ideology always develops against the background of a given ideological field. It was the study of the 'young' Marx which led Althusser to emphasise the self-determining nature of ideology. The dominant ideology is autonomous within the limits imposed by the system of relations of production, and above all, functions at a symbolic level. In this sense, it is never the direct reflection of the system of production which it reaffirms. Its function is to obscure the contradictions of the given system in recreating it at an imaginary level. The determinism to which this ideology is subject is therefore of a negative kind, involving the non-emergence of a specific form of truth. In this sense, the dominant ideology is both mystified and mystifying. It is mystified because it can provide answers only to pseudo-problems. It is mystifying because the kind of understanding which is elaborated inevitably prevents genuine knowledge which would make the dominated classes refuse and reject a given system of relations of production.

The problem which is raised by the analysis of a society in terms of relations of production is that of the range of the explanations given. The basic question is whether such an analysis constitutes a sufficient basis to render intelligible the totality of relationships within a social system. We believe that it does not. Admittedly, it is relevant to an essential characteristic of modern capitalist societies; the relations of production have a direct or indirect influence on the totality of the social interactions which constitute them; and in the struggle with the dominant ideology this analysis inevitably takes priority. This, however, does not mean that it is sufficient in itself. In fact, other divisions besides those based on the relations of production are equally important in determining the dynamics of present-day societies.

Moscovici (1968) has described one such division in his elaboration of the concept of 'natural division'. To make clear its significance, we must first describe what constitutes a 'natural category'; again, the study of human labour is the starting point. By their labour, more precisely by the particular form taken by their relations with nature, men can be divided into 'natural categories'.

Work thus becomes a way of distinguishing between men: men become divided according to whether they have acquired qualifications, in other words, in terms of specific powers and abilities. Although there is a margin for variation in each case, the essential factors are clear. The peasant, the artisan, the engineer or the scientist, has each his own particular sphere. The categories associated with their specialised knowledge are mutually exclusive, although closely interdependent (Moscovici, 1968, p. 61).

The categories thus defined become separated by the process of 'natural division'; this occurs when one mode of exchange between man and the material world is replaced by another mode. Innovations of this kind occurred when, in a world of husbandmen, an artisan class developed, when engineers appeared alongside the artisans, and scientists appeared alongside the engineers. Each of these categories is characterised by a new form of knowledge of its own, a new kind of skill which both transforms and is differentiated from the skill of the preceding category.

The artisan acquires the prescriptions for weaving or the secret of how to choose his clay only from the peasant who weaves or makes pottery. The architect–engineer of the Renaissance was beginning to be able to use books, but it was his attentive observation of the operations of the carpenter or the smith which enabled him to grasp the laws of mechanical force and movement. Invention has often consisted simply in being able to reproduce a work-form in a different context, separated from the customary association with the material work . . . The natural division has its *raison d'être* in the phenomenon to which I have already drawn attention; the institutionalised relation of man to matter is directly mediated by another man. The resulting antagonism is significant and fruitful, for at the same moment the two variants of the same aspect of knowledge meet face to face in concrete form – the husbandman–domestic fabricator and the artisan, the master-mason and the architect–engineer. Each natural category is in some measure a more or less extended transposition of an original category; it is this category transformed. The artisan is the transfigured version of one sector of agricultural activity, the engineer is the new form of one aspect of artisan work, just as the neolithic husbandman, the woman, to be precise, was a revolutionary variant of the hunter and primitive gatherer (Moscovici, 1968, p. 136).

From such a point of view, the division into classes, based on the relations of production, requires a different order of explanation. 'Can we attribute to one and the same cause, i.e. the existence of a surplus, such different effects as the separation into natural categories and the institution of social classes?' (ibid, p. 145). Even though the division into classes is associated with differences in wealth, made possible by a surplus of production, this is not the basis for the process of natural division; on the contrary, the emergence of a new group of producers creates the surplus, the particular distribution of which gives rise to the different classes.

The division of the forces of production into manual workers and intellectuals is thus a complex phenomenon, determined by a number of factors. The need to control ideological production may have meant that the dominant classes first of all selected within their own ranks, or later tried to assimilate, certain categories of 'intellectual' workers by offering them very favourable conditions of work. Moscovici (ibid, p. 10), also sees this as the effect of a 'natural division'.

The separation of workers into 'manual' and 'brain' workers, into those who do and those who direct, preserves a distance which tends to perpetuate itself, the children of each category following the occupation of their parents and reaping the advantages or disadvantages of their position. A different way of sharing wealth would not really be effective in eliminating the consequences of this situation. We should have to transform the work itself by acting upon the totality and structure of knowledge gained up to that point. In short, the solution lies in the discovery of new abilities, a different system of production and different relations with materials.

Some of the conditions which lead to racial or social discrimination are directly related to the system of relations of production. But all cases of discrimination cannot be explained in this way. Thus Rex (1969, p. 147), listing situations which lead to discrimination, puts at the head of his list 'the situation of culture contact between peoples with an advanced industrial and military technology, and hunters, pastoralists and agriculturalists at lower levels of development'. This does not mean that such differentiation may not reinforce an existing class antagonism, in the Marxist sense, or vice versa.

At the sociological level, an analysis based on a study of the relations of production thus needs to be complemented at another level. In the explanatory model which they propose, Marxist authors deliberately leave out any notion of subject or actor; the class struggle is the moving force of history. 'History is indeed a "process without Subject or End(s)", of which the given *circumstances*, in which "men" act as subjects under the determination of social relations, are the product of the *class struggle*. History thus does not

have, in the philosophical sense of the term, a Subject, but
a *motor*, the class struggle' (Althusser, 1973, p. 76). Even
if history took no account of 'subjects' and consisted entirely
of the development of social relations, there would nevertheless still be the subjects or individuals, the men who
interact even although they belong to different groups or
classes. There are the workers and there is the collectivity
of workers. How can these two notions be brought together?
Once more we come up against the need for a study of the
integration between individual and group, between psychological and sociological. We shall return to this question in
the next chapter.

EFFECTIVENESS OF IDEOLOGY

The role of ideologies in the reproduction of relations of
production has been described. They also play a large part
in other aspects of the dynamics of social systems. Thus,
the natural divisions described by Moscovici are accompanied by a system of justificatory and explanatory representations. Even the oldest mythologies bear traces of this. In
this sense, they are even more 'sociological' than epics and
legends.

We must now indicate some of the mechanisms by which
ideologies fulfil their role. Three of these mechanisms will
be examined, although it is not implied that they all operate,
in the same way, in different historical conditions. In fact,
the role which an ideology plays in a social system determines
the ways in which it functions. Thus, of the three mechanisms which we shall describe, the first seems more
characteristic of the functioning of the ideology of modern
societies, while the other two have more general relevance.

Effects of universality and isolation

Poulantzas (1973) has well described the mechanism by
which the social system based upon capitalist relations of
production retains its cohesion. It is paradoxically by an

isolation effect that the State, by presenting itself as the representative of the general interest and will of the people-nation, conceals from the economic agents their class nature by bestowing a false equality upon them. Citizens are set up as individuals with private competing and divergent economic interests, among which the State acts as arbiter. The real contradictions are concealed under the universality of a definition which strips individuals of their economic determination and their place in the relations of production. This ideological definition of the citizen lies behind the working of the legal system. Everyone is equal in the eyes of the law. This 'truth', elevated into a constitutional principle, hides the basic inequality of social classes and does not prevent codes of law from giving more protection to property than to labour, to the proprietor of the means of production than to the worker.

Marx, in the '18th Brumaire', denounces the iniquitous part played by the individualisation of collective relations: according to Marx, it was just this stratagem on the part of the dominant ideology which deprived the French proletariat of victory in the Revolution. Just as Freud, starting from individual psychology, is obliged to acknowledge the importance of the group, Marx, starting from the sociological standpoint, has to acknowledge the individual and his private life. Freud explains collective phenomena in terms of processes concerned with the individual or with the relations between individuals. Marx explains the individual in terms of sociological processes.

So the fact that Marx uses the category of private to mean the isolation of the economic struggle in no way implies a distinction between the private sphere of economic individuals/subjects and the political sphere; rather, it indicates that the isolation of the whole series of socio-economic relations is an effect of the juridical and the ideological (Poulantzas, 1973, p. 132).

The individual is thus defined in ideological terms according to which he represents a negation of social determinism. By means of this negation, the establishing of the individual enables the social to function. Althusser (1970) develops this notion of the integration of individual and group functioning. He defines the individual essentially as an entity subject to obligation, on the basis of demands formulated by ideological agencies such as the family, the church and the school.

There may also be contradictions among the different social groups in power. Ideology must further obscure these contradictions by attributing their historic and universal role to the different factions. This function of ideology characterised Fascist Germany and Italy and facilitated the 'unnatural' alliance between the industrial upper middle class and the great land-owners on the one hand, and the lower middle class and the rural working classes on the other. According to Poulantzas (1974, p. 246), such an alliance was never based on the economic interests of all the parties concerned.

Even apart from the role of ideology in 'unifying' its different 'factions', which are particularly subject to illusions because of their economic position. . . because of the resulting isolation, ideology plays a decisive role: *the petty bourgeoisie literally feeds on the ideology which cements it.* Particularly in Italy, this class was one of the main 'economic' victims of fascism, which bled it white – yet it was the only class to support it *en masse* to the end, and it did so for ideological reasons. This gives some indication of the magnitude of the Comintern's mistake in expecting fascism to fall quickly, because of its 'internal contradictions', or more precisely, because the mass of the petty bourgeoisie would themselves turn from fascism when they found it damaging to their economic interests.

The dominant ideology succeeded in imposing its will on the opposing ideologies by providing a referential model. A further manifestation of the universality effect is therefore the mirror-image effect, by which the ideology of the dominant classes superimposes itself upon those of the dominated classes. Demands for a 'genuine' democracy, for 'real' equality, for an equal right to progress are still ways of participating in the dominant rule of law.

The effect of universality can also be seen in the capacity for recuperation on the part of the dominant ideology. By divesting them of their meaning and detaching them from their original ideological context, it is possible to integrate symbols, ideas or topics which derive from opposing perspectives. Thus a kind of technocratic language, dealing with social injustices, presents them as accidents due to malfunctioning, to be put right by the progress and natural development of current societies. This kind of view gives meaning to the contradictions and conflicts of a society without indicating their real origin. It deprives those who are directly concerned of their main weapon.

Effect of category division

If the ascendancy of the dominant ideology is as strong as is indicated by the description of the effects of the universality and isolation which provide its principal mechanisms, how can we account for the possibility of struggle and of ideological opposition? According to traditional Marxist theory, it is contradictions at the economic level which, in the last resort, allow oppositions to develop at the ideological level. More generally, the existence of groups against which society discriminates may mean that these groups come to reject the 'universal' ideology and put forward an opposing counter-ideology. The strength of this opposing ideology develops as the awareness of the experience of discrimination coincides with knowledge of the objective causes behind such discrimination. Thus ideology becomes practical awareness.

When the worker knows himself as a commodity his knowledge is practical. That is to say, this knowledge brings about an objective, structural change in the object of knowledge. In this consciousness and through it the special objective character of labour as a commodity, its 'use-value' (i.e. its ability to yield surplus produce) which like every use-value is submerged without a trace in the quantitative exchange categories of capitalism, now awakens and becomes social reality (Lukács, 1971, p. 169).

Vidal (1971), at the time of the events of May 1968 in France, was able to make a real-life study of the function of ideology in a situation of emerging awareness. He describes how different ideologies can develop on the basis of the contradictions which appear in a work contract. The so-called reformist ideology, which is fed by the dominant ideology, does not relate experienced contradictions at the work level to the impossibility of properly integrating a group of workers into the established social system. 'Radical' ideology, on the other hand, does associate local contradictions with the impossibility of a satisfactory integration of the workers into the social system as a whole. This latter view facilitates the creation of a representation of society in which antagonistic groups are inevitably opposed. Such a representation reflects the Marxist conceptual framework, in which a distinction is made between productive forces and ownership of the means of production.

The question which must now be asked concerns the nature of this ideological dichotomisation, which arises from the need to distinguish between opponents and allies in the struggle, but which involves the coincidence of theoretical distinctions and actually existing divisions. A theoretical distinction which makes social reality intelligible cannot be found as such in any given situation. The strict application of the theses of historical materialism does not, in all circumstances, exclude the possibility that actual individuals may be assigned to the two classes of production which are distinguished in theory. An operation which is theoretically possible, however, is not necessarily ideologically possible.

Ethnologists have several times been confronted with an analogous problem, and we shall refer to some of these in order to understand better the working of the category division as an ideological mechanism. Jaulin (1973), in his book *Gens de soi, gens de l'autre*, describes the contradictions in category memberships which can be found in certain societies. The author's objections to the structuralist theory of Lévi-Strauss are well-known. In an actual study, reported in the book referred to, of the kinship systems of an African tribe and an Amazon tribe, Jaulin agrees that structuralist formulations may indeed explain a large number of cases of kinship ties; a thorough analysis of the remaining cases, however, shows that ecological factors, which are not taken into consideration by the dichotomies of the structuralist model, are also important and make the reality more complex than might be implied by the rules deduced by the ethnologist from the terms used by the natives. This provides a further example of the fact that ideological, or theoretical, functioning does not necessarily recapture the complexity of reality.

If we carry simplification to the limit, we might say that there is no such thing as an abstraction, because this is never a revelation, but a simplification, or a combination of concrete operations and states, when it is not, first and foremost, a procedure which makes artificial the relation of man to his fellow man and to the world. This is the kind of thing which constitutes the abstraction of the western world (Jaulin, 1973, p. 328).

Starting from a myth which holds that there is incompatibility between two centres of power, that of the tribal chief and that of the war chief, which are nevertheless articulated in the same society, Sebag (1964, p. 162) writes similarly. 'The myth is thus a good representation of the difference between the two forms of sovereignty, but the way in which it represents this difference is not wholly implicit in the actual organization of power. The logical schema to which it refers has a kind of autonomy which an analysis of the infrastructure does not take into account.'

Lévi-Strauss (1963, p. 131) has considered the same problem. 'We are led to conceive of social structures as entities independent of men's consciousness of them (although they in fact govern men's existence), and thus as different from the image which men form of them as physical reality is different from our sensory perceptions of it and our hypotheses about it.' And he also, before these critical remarks, talks of dualistic representations with respect to social systems which are not necessarily dualistic. 'Why do societies affected by a high degree of endogamy so urgently need to

mystify themselves and see themselves as governed by exog-
amous institutions, classical in form, of whose existence they
have no direct knowledge?' (ibid.). The answer can be found
in the principle of 'dualist organisation', which in the last
analysis refers to 'certain fundamental structures of the
human mind, rather than to some privileged region of the
world or to a certain period in the history of civilisation'
(Lévi-Strauss, 1969, p. 75).

The problems raised by the 'universalist' nature of the
explanation will be considered later. Let us for the moment
simply remember that the mechanism of category division
is not a feature only of present-day societies in crisis. The
dualist view seems indeed to be one of the relatively autonomous processes which govern the dynamics of ideology.
We shall show in the penultimate chapter that this 'logical
schema' constitutes in fact an important social psychological
process which makes possible the integration of the individual and the social, and of psychological and sociological
types of explanation.

The effect of social reification

Ideology supports, orients and justifies the practice of a
social system. Its primary function is to relate social action
to the past and to the future; it constitutes the bond between
present and future. Myths have often in this way related the
events and institutions of the present to the great originating
'ideological events'. Certain modern ideologies pay more
attention to the future in their systems of representations;
according to some (Von Rad, 1960) the essential contribution
of Judeo-Christian culture to Western civilisation is to be
found in this reorientation. Even in our time, however,
ideologies oriented toward the past are not lacking. There
are, for example, the dominant ideologies of the South
African Whites as described by Thion (1969). The importance assumed in this ideology by the notions of Trek
(migration), Laager (camp), Republiek (republic) and Voor-
vader (forebears) represents the equivalent of the reappear-

ance of a myth of the Golden Age. Thion does not hesitate to compare this ideology with the Biblical myth of the crossing of the wilderness. It might equally well be compared with the cinema myth of the 'Western'. The future may be practically absent from the ideology of the South Africans, but it occupies an important place in certain religious ideologies of the Blacks of the same country, who project into times to come a type of society contrary to the existing one – in the future society, work will be abolished, wealth will be inexhaustible, the Blacks will be the masters and the Whites will be banished. It therefore seems, and is further indicated by the extraordinary ideological and eschatological notions of some Jewish societies around the beginning of our era, that a situation where there is a dominated people who have scarcely any way of intervening actively and effectively in their social environment, favours the growth of Utopian ideologies. The various forms of African messianism represent manifestations of a similar ideological activity. These ideologies, although not concerned with direct intervention in the 'real' world may nevertheless lay the foundations for such intervention.

Those considerations do not mean that a narrow functionalism is appropriate to the explanation of ideologies. Frequently, social systems or groups for which it would be advantageous to take a limited time perspective, favour a form of Utopian illusionism. We may refer, with Poulantzas (1974), to the example of the Third International confronted with Fascism. As the economic crisis of the thirties developed, the Comintern strengthened its belief in a speedy victory for the proletariat. Fascism was thus able to reinforce its position while the Communist International persisted in rejecting any alliance with the social democrats.

It would also be wrong to retain a definition of ideology which presented it simply as an entity without substance. One aspect of the functioning of an ideology is precisely its capacity for self fulfilment. This effect can be clearly seen in the relations between dominant and dominated groups. The images which the former project onto the latter most frequently tend to justify the elimination of the latter in economic, sexual or political competition. Currently, the members of dominated groups are defined as unfitted to carry out certain functions. This legal or informal edict means that the dominated are not properly prepared for the assumption of certain tasks, and this is then claimed as justification for their elimination. Circular argument may be a bad thing, but it may still contribute toward the creation of reality.

Ethnologists have also been interested in this effect of social reification. In 1971, at a conference on Racism at UNESCO entitled 'Race and Culture', Lévi-Strauss developed the thesis that, even though the influence of racial factors on cultural products was not satisfactorily demonstrated, cultural factors (such as the laws of marriage and the rules concerning discrimination) do indeed mean that ethnic groups exist as such. He had already written, 'An anthropologist who tries to interpret the evolution of human races and sub-races as though it were simply the result of natural conditions, would enter the same blind alley as a zoologist attempting to explain the present differences among dogs by purely biological or ecological considerations, without taking human intervention into account' (1963, p. 385). It is by means of representations and rules which justify differentiation among groups, that these groups become or remain an aspect of reality which even physiology has to take account of.

Ideological influences are equally real and important at the level of social institutions. There is no kind of institutionalised social relationship which is not affected by ideology; it conditions even relations between man and woman, and between parents and children. Ideology exercises its influence mainly through language. It would be pointless to try to make different ideological languages into directly corresponding systems of representations which simply reflect a different kind of reality in one particular way. Ideological languages construe specific forms of reality. In this context, Sebag (1964) writes, a myth is the kind of thing which can give the impression that events which are essentially beyond its scope do in fact fall within its orbit; but this transformation can only come about in so far as it rests upon the real knowledge of human existence which is reflected in the symbolic system. The externality of the expression in relation to the meaning in no way excludes the possibility that, once it has taken shape, it may become a primary means of access to this meaning for those in the know. If we render ineffective the languages which form the basis of human existence, human existence itself will become uncertain.

To summarise the last few lines, if we discount the ideologies underlying social institutions, these institutions themselves will be in danger.

The blueprint mediated by revolutionary ideology likewise represents an attempt to realise ideological notions. The revolution represents an attempt to recreate society as a whole. 'By denying even temporarily the existing hierarchies, by integrating what in the old world was diverse and opposed, it tends to abolish everything which does not emerge from its own will, and to make society a genuine unity in so far as it is as a whole underpinned by a unique orientation toward the future' (ibid, p. 182). We must seek there the explanation of the rigour which is essential to any realisation of a revolutionary design. 'What is involved is simply the problem of aligning the total pattern of social life with the political blueprint which, like any such blueprint, treats all the items with which reality provides it, as so many signs to which a series of operations may profitably be attached'. (ibid, p. 183). Sebag, aware of the lack of correspondence between a society and the image it creates of itself, likewise admits that the carrying out of a plan is never a complete success.

The decentring of expression in relation to meaning seems to us to imply that a society is never what it says it is, that there is an unbridgeable gap between its picture of itself and the reality, which derives from the very laws of symbolism. But think what is required by the alternative possibility, i.e. the attempt to transform a human collectivity by making it fit a conceptual schema which by definition cannot be homogeneous in its application (ibid, p. 183).

SCIENCE AND IDEOLOGY

Ideology is relevant in the most varied fields of social action. It is also relevant at the scientific level. Certain forms of activity, which are regarded by some as scientific, are regarded by others as the product of ideology. Thus Herbert (1966, p. 165) refuses the designation of 'science' to the fields of knowledge with which we are concerned in this book.

It may therefore be said that, *in their present state*, the mixed bag of psychology, sociology and social psychology has failed to produce any scientific knowledge at all (since by any standards, the 'realisation of reality' does not constitute a scientific equivalent of the methodical accumulation of knowledge) and that, on the contrary, these fields of study currently provide an ideology which reflects social practice throughout the world. They show, unintentionally, the ideological core in the complex whole, in the form of fragmentary discourse with a kind of neurotic coherence, supporting a specific function in relation to the complex structured whole.

This raises the problem of the relations between, and the possible distinction between, ideology and science. Writers like Althusser (1969) seem to make a clear distinction between ideology and science. In fact, however, it is difficult to decide whether the practice of the human sciences is more relevant to science or ideology; the problem involves the nature of the links between the two kinds of activity. Scientific activity is virtually an operation by which ideological realities are transformed.

In this context, we should remember the model of the three generalities sketched by Althusser (1969). Generality I 'constitutes the raw material that the science's theoretical practice will transform into specified "concepts"...the raw material on which the labour of science is expended...its particular labour consists of *elaborating its own* scientific facts through a critique of the *ideological 'facts'* elaborated by an earlier ideological theoretical practice' (ibid, p. 184). Generality III is obtained by transformation of generality I. Such transformations are achieved by means of theoretico-technical mechanisms (generality II), described as follows.

Constituted by the corpus of concepts whose more or less contradictory unity constitutes the 'theory' of the science at the (historical) moment under consideration, the 'theory' that defines the field in which all the problems of the science must necessarily be posed (that is, where the difficulties met by the science in its object, in the confrontation of its 'facts' and its 'theory', of its previous knowledge and its 'theory', or of its 'theory' and its new knowledges, will be posed in the form of a problem by and in this field). We must rest content with these schematic gestures and not enter into the dialectic of this theoretical labour. They will suffice for an understanding of the fact that theoretical practice produces Generalities iii by the work of Generality ii on Generality i (ibid, pp. 184–5).

Similarly, according to Piaget, knowledge, at least in its operational form, is an internalised (symbolic) and reversible operation carried out on reality. The cognitive structures which he studies are systems of transformations which enable us to transcend the limitations of particular centrations and points of view not integrated with each other. Piaget has been primarily concerned to describe the work of transformation of which the child becomes capable in the course of his development, in relation to the knowledge of physical reality. But Piaget's epistemological thesis is in fact that science develops according to the same laws as are revealed by the study of the ontogenetic development of knowledge.

It is only by considering, as these two authors do, scientific activity as a work of transformation of partial truths into more general truths, that we can distinguish among different activities in the manipulation of knowledge. In fact, technical activities and some forms of magic may equally imply the exercise of rigorous logic and produce effects at the level of physical or social reality. Both start from 'established' truths but, unlike scientific activity, their aim is not to create new truths by integrating or bringing together old truths. Technicians and priests reproduce truths without reorganising them in a fundamental or critical way.

Ideology also works with established truths, but does not constitute a fixed body of knowledge. The system of relations of production develops, and the dominant ideology which justifies it is transformed as a result. Again, the conflict between dominant ideologies and opposing ideologies reveals the internal contradictions of the former and ensures their further development. From this point of view, the task of ideology seems very like the task of science. This is purely a matter of superficial appearance; in fact, when science feels the need to go beyond contradictions at the theoretical level and integrate provisional truths and more general truths, there will be an effort by scientists or by others to carry out experiments and create techniques which will provide evidence in favour of these new truths. As far as the dominant ideology is concerned, theoretical activity is generally limited to purely symbolic assimilation which, for good reasons, envisages only very limited changes in the ways in which a society functions. The dominant ideology is literally encapsulated in an existing state of affairs. When it finds itself confronted with changes which cannot be accommodated within its limits, it takes refuge in an illusionary reintegration which retains only such aspects of the new reality as support its outmoded position. It is the function of the opposing ideology to propose radical practical changes which alone can bear witness to the justice of its position. Thus, by definition, the ideology of the dominated groups is more scientific than the dominant ideology.

The distinctions between ideologies and scientific activities are unquestionably theoretical. They serve the function of making intelligible an extremely complex reality in which both ideology and science combine to provide multiply determined meanings. While it is true that the ideologies of contemporary society have to assimilate the results of scientific activity in one way or another, it is also true that this does not take place in an ideological vacuum. Sometimes science advances as a direct result of ideological pressures. This means that it has to produce limited areas of knowledge which do not question but rather reinforce a certain view of the world. Bourgeois societies cannot be completely a-scientific or anti-scientific. On the contrary, their establishment on the basis of a partial rejection of religious and feudal societies was made possible by recourse to a scientific universe of discourse. It is therefore natural that they should have recourse to scientific activity in order to maintain themselves.

The effects of ideology on scientific activity are often negative in the sense that some levels of analysis cannot be approached. For example, this is probably the reason for the unwillingness to study certain social determinants of intellectual development. The fact is that the demonstration of new truths at this level could readily lead to the questioning of the traditional working of education, the ideological role of which is important. Thus there arises the need for a form of scientific activity which will escape from ideological constraints and avoid the pitfalls of reductionism. Explanation at one level does not necessarily exclude explanations at other levels. It may be true that the study of intellectual development, at the individual level, represents an important scientific contribution; but it is also true that this development takes place within a network of social interactions. To exclude any consideration of this social context can easily lead to ideological reductionism which, while invoking the principle of spontaneous and autonomous development, tends to justify respect for the established educational order.

The following represents a further example of reductionist determination. It is possible to study the disturbed functioning of a work group in terms of the articulation of roles within the group. It would, however, be absurd to restrict oneself to such a study, refusing to take account of the fact that the group forms part of a social system which renders meaningful the division of labour within the group concerned.

Omission or reductionism constitutes an important mechanism by which ideology influences science. Unjustified generalisation is simply the other side of this same mechanism. It consists of advancing as a complete explanation what is relevant only to one particular aspect of reality.

Affectivity no doubt is involved in all forms of social behaviour. A whole field of applied psychology, called group
dynamics, has developed, to sensitise people, who meet in
an unstructured situation, to the affective aspects of the
social interactions in which they take part. We do not
pretend to pass judgment here upon the scientific value of
this line of activity, but some other recent approaches, such
as those described and criticised by Pagès, have been
directed toward a different end. Pagès, as a practitioner of
the techniques of sensitization, raises the question of the
political significance which such techniques may assume in
certain situations. 'The group aims would seem also to have
political significance for the society as a whole. They may
act to support basic social structures, especially the image
of a united society and the validity of a social hierarchy,
based on the conviction that there is a class of persons
who (for the good of all, of course) are entitled to direct
others...' (Pagès, 1971–2, p. 301). The one-sided interpretation of reality on the basis of affectivity may indeed serve
to justify the established order, even though it obscures or
denies the economic conflicts which characterise our societies. 'Is it not one of the functions of group dynamics to
show Americans how pleasant the world they live in is, how
stupid they would be to want to change it, and to encourage
people from other countries to accept it?...My hypothesis
here is that the culture of the group at Bethel fulfils the
political function of preserving American society from
internal and external disruption' (ibid).

Together with the more direct influences exerted by
ideology on scientific output, we must also allow of the
existence of indirect influences, more difficult to trace, of
which we may mention especially omission and unjustified
generalisation. These various influences explain why scientific productivity becomes the object of a struggle between
the forces which constitute a society. They also explain how
the agents of scientific production, independently of their
own awareness, occupy a particular position in their social
system. It is important for them, then, as citizens and as

scientists, to define the political significance of their work in a political and social whole. Such an awareness, a product of collective effort, is an indispensable condition for scientists to control the ideological determinants of their own work. In fact, the scientific world is composed of groups with different, opposing or competing approaches. It also reflects, at this level, a conflict between different centrations, which, by explanation and confrontation, leads to new knowledge. A development such as this does not take place without stagnation, retreat and impasse, which may be taken advantage of by ideological determinism. The dynamic of scientific activity is essentially social. The positions which scientific teams feel obliged to take admittedly derive from the development and verification or rejection of hunches, hypotheses and counter-hypotheses. But they are also products of a social dynamic described by Lemaine (Lemaine, Matalon and Provansal, 1969; Lemaine and Kastersztein, 1971–2) which leads to differentiations and oppositions in the course of 'the struggle for life in the scientific world'.

The reader acquainted with empirical research in sociology will probably be surprised by the almost total absence of reference to this work. We have deliberately chosen not to follow the same approach for sociology as for psychology. The present work in fact had its basis in psychology, and was primarily concerned to show that psychology itself was insufficient for the study of the specialised field of group relations. As far as the sociological approach is concerned, we simply wished to indicate its distinctive position and its difference from the psychological approach, by showing that its goal is to put forward conceptual systems relevant to the functioning of society. The representations which the groups in a society entertain of themselves and of other groups have an important role in the foundation of a social system. They are, however, apprehended at the individual level. Once again, then, we encounter the need for some kind of integration of psychological and sociological.

3

The social psychological approach

Neither psychology nor sociology provides a complete explanation of the reality which they study. This is not because they are insufficiently developed, but because each of these approaches includes in its explanatory system, rarely explicitly but frequently implicitly, notions developed by the other approach. We may wonder, then, how the two approaches manage to enjoy a measure of autonomy. Devereux (1972) has tried to answer this question, and we shall first give an account of his views on the integration of psychology and sociology. Piaget (1965) was also concerned with the relations between the two types of explanation; according to him, there is an analogy between psychological and sociological which becomes a form of isomorphism in the study of the relations between social logic and individual logic.

After considering these two theoretical attempts to resolve the problem, we shall outline some examples of genuinely social psychological, experimental studies. These will show how the experimental creation of different conditions of interaction between individuals creates forces which can be observed through performance, representations and judgments, and which are neither purely individual nor purely sociological, but reflect the integration between the individual and the existing social reality. The validity and generality of the processes thus revealed will be discussed at the end of the chapter.

IRREDUCIBLE AND COMPLEMENTARY UNIVERSES
OF DISCOURSE

The psychologist is concerned with the study of processes
at the individual level, the sociologist with the functioning
of society. At these two levels, it is the function of science
to transform the pre-scientific or ideological truths of
common sense, which often represent simply restatements,
at the imaginary level, of matters of fact. The stability of
these new scientific constructions, however, only holds for
the level at which they were developed. Beyond this, they
lose meaning. This position is defended by Devereux (1972,
p. 18). ' "Society" (and "culture" and "psyche"), in the first
instance do no more than provide tentative explanations.
But, once they are "construed" (though not reified), these
explanations – which in fact simply define perspectives –
may themselves constitute explanatory frames of reference
which are both self-sufficient and valid...but only as long
as we do not lose sight of their explanatory "origin".'

The irreducibility of the two systems of explanation means
that we have two different universes of discourse, both of
which cannot be used at the same time. This leads to the
principle of complementarity between the two explanations,
according to which one must carry each explanation to the
limit of its usefulness; what remains must then be explained
in terms of the other level of explanation. This complemen-
tarist view of the integration between two levels of explanation may, however, be stated in more precise terms for
psychology and sociology; what is an ' operant motive' at one
level becomes an 'instrumental motive' at the other. An
example of this kind of complementarity is given by Devereux in his study of the fighters in the Hungarian rebellion
of 1956. A whole range of subjective motives, not necessarily
having anything to do with the social problems of the time,
led people to participate in the revolt.

'Si bis faciunt idem, non est idem' (if two people do the same
thing, it is not necessarily the same thing). Where one man revolts
because he had been exploited, another because, twelve years

earlier, the Russians had raped his wife, another because he hates all authority, still another may revolt because he wishes to impress his girl friend with his patriotism and valour. All these men may fight with equal ardour, kill an equal number of secret police and Russians, and therefore achieve *militarily and socially identical results. Psychologically, however, the results may not be the same.'* (Devereux, 1961, p. 235).

In this example, with all of the particular interpretations of which we do not agree – the 'social' effect of an act, for example, is not necessarily independent of the meaning which the individual actor gives it – the various motives operating at the psychological level were able to find suitable expression in one single collective social movement of revolt which thus provided them with an instrumental motive. Conversely, for anyone studying the insurrection movement at the sociological level, the operant motives of the psychological level become instrumental motives. And so, although the sociological and psychological universes of discourse may each be irreducible, they are not without mutual relevance.

In addition to instrumentality, there are other connections. Devereux further states that 'were anthropologists to draw up a complete list of all known types of cultural behaviour, this list would overlap, point by point, with a similarly complete list of impulses, wishes, fantasies, etc., obtained by psychoanalysts in a clinical setting, thus demonstrating, by identical means and simultaneously, the psychic unity of mankind and the validity of psychoanalytic interpretations of culture' (Devereux, 1976, pp. vi–vii). The justification for this psychoanalytic interpretation of culture is based on the notion 'that material repressed in our society may be conscious and culturally implemented in another society' (ibid, p. 85). That is possible because the psychic unity of the human race encompasses the possibility of a very high degree of variation on the basis of limited potentiality. Devereux thus rejects the existence of archetypes in Jung's sense.

In support of his ethnopsychoanalytic thesis, Devereux

(1972) refers to his investigations of abortion in primitive societies. He lists the psychological motives for abortion as indicated in psychoanalytic literature, under several general headings, and presents an exhaustive classification of the practice and models of abortion in 400 populations, concluding, 'So far as we have been able to ascertain, our ethnological data do not contain any trait which does not have a counterpart in some clinically reported and theoretically explained fantasy' (Devereux, 1976, p. 88). Note that at the psychoanalytic level, studies were not carried out on the same populations, but reference was made simply to material collected by psychoanalysts in Western societies.

The view that there are relations between the unconscious and culture is obviously relevant to the position that psychological and sociological explanations are not mutually interchangeable. A psychological product may, in the same or in a different population, become an institution or social practice – perhaps through the principle of instrumentality which we have described. It is however not permissible

to allow the transposition of conceptual models pertaining to the individual to the socio-cultural system as a whole, and the interpretation of the socio-cultural structure and process *purely* in terms of the psychology of the individual, even if he does happen to belong to the society whose structure and process one 'interprets'. Specifically, and in simplest terms, the Constitution of the United States *is* not and can never *be* the 'superego' or the 'ego-ideal' of American society. Moreover, it can never *function* in that capacity within that – or any other – society, for the good and sufficient reason that society does not have a superego or an ego-ideal, any more than the psyche of an individual has a Constitution or a Supreme Court. What can and does happen, is that a particular individual may *incorporate* into his psyche – but only in the form of *psychological materials* – certain aspects of his society and culture (Devereux, 1961, p. 233).

Devereux does not therefore integrate psychology and sociology as closely as some Freudian-Marxists or ethno-Freudians tend to do. Roudinesco (1973) criticises these two forms of reductionism. The Freudian-Marxists, of whom Reich is a protagonist, are too ready to assimilate, by way of what we have called reductionism and unjustified generalisation, 'unconscious repression and social repression, a psychological process of an essentially internal nature and an aspect of ideology of an essentially external nature' (Roudinesco, 1973, p. 28). The exponents of Freudian anthropology, for their part, too often neglect socio-economic factors in their explanation of the workings of primitive societies. Thus Roudinesco (ibid, p. 41) writes of Roheim,

Overlooking the fact that the axe is both a phallic symbol and a primary tool of human economy, he makes the mistake of denying the determining power of economic organisation in favour of the kind of explanation which ultimately has recourse to myths, dreams and fantasies. If the 'utilitarian' function of the tool is regarded as secondary to its primary symbolic function, the discussion of 'the nature of the axe' reflects a kind of mysticism and we may have to contemplate an explanation of human evolution in terms of religion and mythology.

Let us take Devereux's point that psychological and sociological explanations, although mutually relevant, cannot be reduced to one or the other. But, since they are mutually relevant, the task of social psychology is precisely to study these aspects of mutual relevance, and work out their implications in specific terms, while respecting the autonomy of both psychology and sociology.

PIAGETIAN ANALOGIES AND ISOMORPHISMS

Where Devereux rejects 'the transposition of conceptual models pertaining to the individual to the socio-cultural system as a whole' (Devereux, 1961, p. 233) Piaget has no hesitation in doing so when he develops a strict parallelism between psychological explanation and sociological explanation.

Three classes of ideas must therefore be distinguished in sociological explanation (as indeed in psychological explanation); there are causal acts, the operations which enable these acts to be carried out by systematising them, and ideological factors (comparable to introspective or egocentric factors in psychology) which distort perspectives when such socio-centric symbolism is not dissociated from genuinely operational mechanisms (Piaget, 1965, p. 60).

A structural analogy is developed with the three psychological levels. Sensory-motor thinking, symbolic thinking and operational thinking are compared to the technical, ideological and scientific activities which operate at the sociological level. This analogy casts light upon the question of relations between infrastructure and superstructure.

Just as psychology has come to recognise that the content of consciousness can offer no kind of causal explanation and that the only possible causal explanation must be in terms of behaviour, i.e. action, so sociology, in discovering the relativity of the superstructures with respect to the infrastructures, has recourse to explanations of ideology in terms of action – communal actions carried out to ensure the continuation of the social group in a given material environment; active, technical actions, which are perpetuated in collective representations, rather than being derived from them in the form of application (ibid, p. 21).

As is the case in psychology, the sociological superstructure comprises different levels.

Sooner or later, sociology introduces into the kinds of common or differentiated thinking which it is concerned to explain, a distinction analogous to that made in the individual field, between egocentric or subjective thinking and decentred or objective thinking; it has to be recognised that certain forms of thought reflect the preoccupations of the sub-group to which the individual belongs. . . on the other hand, it also indicates, on the basis of other approaches, the possibility of a genuine universalisation of the operations involved, as represented by scientific thinking (ibid, p. 26).

What is involved is not, therefore, a straightforward analogy between psychology and sociology; no more than suggestions for causal relations are given. To demonstrate the case, we must develop another analogy based on a less well-known book by Piaget and Inhelder (1971) on mental images. Mental images are representations of reality, based on perceptions, which constitute a supporting framework for the operations of concrete thinking. Mental images do not take account of the autonomous development of operational structures. The latter are essentially transformational systems which can be understood in terms of axiomatic logic; the former are more limited systems which lack operational reversibility. In the course of development, however, mental images partake more and more of the characteristics of certain forms of intellectual development. Indeed, they may serve as representatives of the different stages of operational transformations. If in children at the preoperational stage, thinking depends mainly on mental images, it is because preoperational thinking can never transform images. At this stage of thinking, the appreciation of details is more important than the understanding of transformations; images direct thought. This is no longer so at the operational level at which thought transforms images. Consider the case of children who think that a line is longer than a parallel line simply because the end of one line comes beyond the end of the other, without regard to the starting point of the two lines. Here,

two attitudes come into play: (a) a general attitude of an ordinal (not yet metric) character, that obviously derives from notional activity, and (b) representational centration on finishing rather than starting points, in which the image appears to play an important part. Indeed, representational centration on the finishing point indicates primacy of the state over movement, or the primacy of what is absolute over what is relative (between starting and finishing points). And this primacy of the absolute state is the result of the 'cinematographic process' characteristic of the image (Piaget and Inhelder, 1971, p. 334).

Mental images do not, then, by themselves, provide the basis for adequate knowledge. It is operational thinking which, by integrating successive stages, leads to knowledge and thereby to the possibility of anticipatory and adaptive images. Thinking is thus not just a reflection of reality. It develops on the basis of images which in the first place act to limit its influence but which are ultimately co-ordinated by it. At the sociological level, ideology is the theoretical factor which corresponds to images at the psychological level. Ideological representations of social reality are not themselves scientific, although they may make possible the scientific activity to which they are subjected. Ideologies, like symbolic thinking and mental images, do not have the advantage of the autonomous development which characterises operational thinking and science. There is thus a structural analogy between the two levels; at both levels a form of structured activity transforms the products of activities which do not themselves show the same structural dynamics.

This finally leads us to consider an even closer link between psychology and sociology, at the level of cognitive structures. We may ask how such structures originate. The work of the Geneva school demonstrates the defensibility of a psychological study of the problem. We may, however, refer to a relevant argument by Devereux (1972, p. 9).

According to Poincaré, if a phenomenon is amenable to one explanation, it is also amenable to various other explanations, just as adequate as the first explanation to illuminate the nature of the phenomenon concerned. . . The truth of the matter is that a human phenomenon which can be explained only in one way is, in effect, not explained at all. . . This is perhaps especially the case if the first explanation makes the phenomenon comprehensible, controllable and predictable in terms of its own frame of reference.

Piaget (1965, p. 145) specifically raises the problem of a possible sociological explanation of cognitive operations. 'The aim of these few pages is to re-examine the much-discussed issue of the social or individual nature of logic, taking into account a new fact, the existence of operational "groupings", which developmental psychology finds to play a part in the development of reason.'

The problem is to know whether the individual alone can achieve operational thinking, representing as it does, an organisation of internalised, combinable and reversible actions. Before answering this question, Piaget first shows that there is a correspondence between the genetic development of different forms of cognitive components and that of different forms of social interaction. The simultaneous changes in the two fields when operational thinking is being acquired, are particularly striking.

Corresponding to the operational stage, strictly defined (from 7 to 11 or 12 years of age), there is an equally clear advance in socialisation, whereby the child becomes able to co-operate; this means that the child no longer thinks entirely in terms of himself, but in terms of the co-ordination, actual or possible, of different points of view. In this way he becomes capable of discussion – and of that internalised form of discussion which constitutes reflection – of collaboration and of producing orderly accounts which can be understood by the other party. These collective games have common laws. The understanding at this stage, of the relations of reciprocity (e.g. the inversion of right and left by a person facing himself in a mirror, the co-ordination of spatial perspectives, etc.) shows the generality of these new attitudes and their relation to thinking itself (Piaget, 1965, p. 157).

Is it possible that this correspondence reflects a causal link? For Piaget (ibid, p. 158), there can be no answer to this question. 'Since the two kinds of progress are so closely related, the question seems insoluble, except in so far as one can say that they represent two indissoluble aspects of one form of reality, both social and individual.'

Later in the book, it is stated that certain social relations, which are regarded as acts carried out by certain members of the society with respect to other members, in cases of equilibrium show the same 'logic' as that which governs individual actions. 'Social relations, which are in equilibrium in co-operation, thus consist of "groupings" of operations, just like the logical operations carried out by the individual on the external world, and laws of grouping must eventually define the form of ideal equilibrium for both (ibid, p. 159).

The example given is that of the mechanism of intellectual exchange between individuals. Such exchange presupposes a common system of signs and definitions, but also presupposes conservation of the propositions which have been accepted by those involved in the exchange. This kind of reciprocity and reversibility enables the participants to return to propositions which have been recognised by both parties. Intellectual exchange therefore implies a form of conservation and reversibility. Such conservation and reversibility also apply in the exchange of goods, in relation to defining as 'debt' what is 'credit' for another, and in allowing later reference to these recognised facts. Such exchanges in an equilibrium state form a system of reversible operations, as in operational thinking. Piaget's conclusion (ibid, p. 162) is that 'there turns out to be a functional identity between individual operations, and co-operation in terms of the laws of equilibrium, which encompass both'.

The same kind of logical equilibrium is to be found at the level of inter-individual interaction and at the level of the organisation of individual actions. It may well be thought that such correspondence provides the basis for the integration of individual and group levels. But the isomorphism or identity between individual logic and social logic which are thus asserted might perhaps be restricted to limited and direct interaction between individuals. Are they still to be found when multiple mediations, and more specifically, the ideological representations current within a society, have their part to play? At the end of the text to which we have been referring, Piaget (ibid, p. 162–3) admits that centrations due to egoism and constraint may disturb the equilibrium of social interaction. Elsewhere (Piaget and Weil, 1951), as we have seen, 'sociocentrism' has been invoked to explain the absence of reciprocity behaviour with regard to other national groups. An integration of individual and group must be developed at the level of such centrations. Before showing how this is possible in the particular field of intergroup relations, we must give some examples of experimental studies of socio-psychological integration.

SOCIAL PSYCHOLOGICAL EXPERIMENT

The Piagetian approach to relations between individual and social has not given rise to many empirical investigations (but see Nielsen, 1951). Devereux's theses have been illustrated by psychoanalytic and anthropological studies rather than experimental research. Thus none of the theoretical positions relevant to the integration of the individual and the sociological which we have presented has stimulated a programme of experimental research. We shall now try to show by means of examples that experimental social psychology is well-suited to the investigation of the possibilities of such integration.

Before we actually embark on the field of experimental social psychology, we must first clarify a misunderstanding arising from a form of naturalistic thinking which defines the theoretical position to which any research is relevant, in terms of the number of persons used in the investigation. Experimental social psychology works with limited groups of individuals. Thus, theoretically, it should occupy a place between psychology, which studies individuals, and sociology, which studies social aggregates or societies. Such considerations have led to the role of social psychology being defined as the development of 'intermediate' theories dealing with the face to face interaction of individuals, as opposed to so-called 'macro-sociological' theories dealing with society as a whole. From such a point of view, social psychology would also be concerned with studying the processes characterising the different 'cells' such as the family, the union or fabric of which go to make up society. This kind of notion simply amounts to introducing a third level, between the psychological and the sociological, and leaves unanswered the problem of the integration of the individual with the micro-social on the one hand, and the integration of the micro-social with the macro-social on the other.

Social psychological experimentation, as we conceive it, has no bearing on the micro-sociological. It is concerned with the integration between individual and social, most frequently by studying the interaction of a limited number of individuals. Such interaction enables us to cast light on the processes which constitute the individual, from the social standpoint, and the social from the individual standpoint. In this and the next paragraph, we shall illustrate this position by giving examples of social psychological experiments and paradigms, and at the end of the chapter we shall return to the problems of validity and generality raised by such research.

Questions about the integration of individual and social led Sherif (1935) to devise his famous experiment concerning the influence of the group on the formation of norms and attitudes. The questions which this experiment was designed to answer were as follows. (1) In an unstructured and unpredictable objective situation without norms, will an individual introduce some standard and degree of stability? Will individual norms emerge? (2) In the same fluctuating and unstable situation, what will happen in a group situation where a number of individuals have to give their judgments of the stimulus? Will the judgments of the different individuals be unrelated, or will a common standard be established? Will group norms emerge? (3) When both individual and inter-individual norms develop, how will these be related?

Sherif's attempt to provide an experimental answer to these questions is well-known. In a completely dark room, he showed a tiny point of light for a few seconds, thus creating an ambiguous situation. The point of light, which actually remains stationary seems to move (autokinetic phenomenon), for the subjects have no stabilising frame of reference. When the subjects have to judge the distance the point has moved on each trial when they are alone, their responses at first show a high degree of variability, and then settle down to a much smaller range about a median response; individual norms are thus created. When different subjects, who have established such individual norms, are asked to judge the extent of the movement again, in turn and out loud in the presence of each other, the different individual norms give way to a group norm. The total number of responses takes on a new variability about a new median, common for the whole group. The norm which is thus produced in the group situation persists when, later on, the members of the experimental groups are once again subjected to the experience alone. Sherif thus found that, while individual norms gave way under the impact of social interaction, social norms seemed to have more binding force than individual norms. Further, a social norm constituted an original group product. 'The norm which appears in a group situation is not the mean of the individual norms. It is a resultant which cannot simply be inferred on the basis of the individual positions. It is also necessary to introduce the characteristics peculiar to the particular interaction process which takes place' (Sherif, 1954).

Among the experiments which have investigated the specific characteristics of social interaction, we may refer to that of Sampson (described by Sherif and Sherif, 1969). Sampson uses Sherif's paradigm and articulates the experimental situation with the social relations in which the subjects were already involved before the experiment. According to the nature of these relations, one should find either social elaboration of a new norm or reinforcement of individual norms. By using appropriate techniques, Sampson first studied the social relations between novices and monks in a convent. Then, pairs of subjects were selected, representing typical kinds of relation, in particular, the following: (1) novices during the first week of their stay in the monastery, who had mutual relations of equality (four pairs); (2) novices at the end of their first year between whom there were asymmetrical relations, one of each pair holding the other in higher esteem than he was held in himself (five pairs); (3) novices and monks who differed in status, in addition to which the relation was characterised by ideological and interpersonal conflict (five pairs).

All the pairs first took part in an individual condition and then in a group condition, involving judgment in the autokinetic situation. The formation of inter-individual norms, as predicted, followed a different course in the three experimental conditions. First week novices showed mutual influence and their social norm reflected a compromise between the two pre-existing norms, each member of the pair making similar concessions. In the case of the more experienced novices, the effect of the asymmetrical relations was that the member with the greater esteem, after several concessions, found himself again with his own norm, his partner having joined him meanwhile. Finally, the pairs made up of two members of different status, in conflict, finished up with two norms, the monks retaining their position from the start and the novices, after a few attempts at a rapprochement, returning to their individual norm.

By improving, in an ingenious way, the experimental situation used by Sherif, Lemaine, Lasch and Ricateau (1971–2), in Paris, obtained findings analogous to those of Sampson, manipulating their subjects' perception of ideological differences. Experimental paradigms like those of Sherif do then enable us to study the interaction of individual and social reality by studying certain kinds of judgment.

Another experimental paradigm, relevant to sociopsychological integration in decision-making, emerged from a particular socio-economic context. During the Second World War, the American government wanted to make better use of available food supplies. More specifically, they wanted to get housewives to use more poultry and meat offal. Lewin (1958), arguing that norms emerge at a group level, suggested trying to change eating habits in a group situation. Accordingly, he got together female volunteers from the Red Cross in groups of 13 to 17 persons and tried to change their culinary preferences in two different ways. For one half of the groups, he used the classic method of persuasion. An expert gave a talk, showing how a change in feeding habits could contribute to the war effort and improve the nutritive quality of meals, and also provided recipes for the preparation of the new kinds of meat. For these 'lecture' groups, social interaction was limited. In the other groups, there was more interaction, especially among the different members of the group. After a short introduction on the contribution to the war effort and the dietetic aspects of the proposed change, the participants were invited to give their opinions and to discuss the problem of offal. After a prolonged discussion, a vote was taken in which people promised to prepare at least once during the following week, one of the dishes recommended. All the members of these groups declared themselves ready to try the experiment. Interviews, carried out a week later, confirmed that the 'discussion' method had been much more effective (32 per cent of the housewives having served offal) than the 'lecture' method which was effective for only 3 per cent of the participants. We have indicated elsewhere (Moscovici and Doise, 1974) how more carefully controlled experiments enable us to appreciate more accurately which of these factors – discussion, public commitment or group agreement – were behind the success of the discussion groups.

More recently, studies of risk-taking in groups have given fresh impetus to the study of the relations between discussion, decision, consensus and normative change. Let us note the effect of increasing risk in a group situation as shown by these studies. The experimental procedure, in general, is as follows. The subjects first respond individually to a questionnaire (Kogan and Wallach, 1967) on the risk which should be taken in various situations which are described to them. Then, in groups of four, they are asked to give a common response to the same questions. It has been systematically noted, in different countries and in less hypothetical situations, that group consensus provides more risky decisions than individual responses. No satisfactory explanation of this risk-taking phenomenon has been given. In fact, we have been able to show (Doise and Moscovici, 1973) that this increase in risk represents only a particular case of a more general phenomenon called group polarisation. Groups take decisions which on average are more risky than those taken by individuals and likewise polarise their responses to problems which have nothing to do with risk. To account for this generality, which has since been well authenticated (Moscovici and Doise, 1974), Moscovici and Zavalloni (1969) put forward the notion of normative involvement. In the research on both risk taking and group polarisation, it has been found that response tendencies which are already present in individuals, become even more marked in group interaction. For such accentuation to occur, however, there must be an initial divergence among the members of the group, and they must be able to come to grips with this in a discussion in depth (Moscovici, Doise and Dulong, 1972).

These researches may appear very far removed from the theoretical problems with which we were concerned in the previous pages. This does not seem to us necessarily to represent a process of *décalage* between theory and empirical research. Let us note first of all that these researches are not relevant to the relations between individual and group in the sense that they do not attempt to show that either is derived from the other. Unfortunately, we cannot claim to witness the birth of Aphrodite. Even in the 'individual' conditions in the experiments referred to, the individual is already involved in a network of social relations. It is simply the case that, in these conditions, more scope is left to his individual characteristics and individual style, which itself is the result of previous interactions, and to his own particular way of approaching and structuring a given situation. In the 'group' situation, we are concerned to find out how a number of these individual units interacting produce a new entity. In situations like this, the problem is how a number of individuals, at a given moment in their development, are linked together in a particular social setting presented to them through different experimental situations.

Let us further illustrate our position. An important aspect of the individual and the sociological, as 'acted' in the experiments on group polarisation, is the cognitive aspect. More or less isolated individuals, interacting directly with each other, have to deal with problems. The role of sociological factors will be further illustrated, but it has already been demonstrated that interactions between individuals are affected by the relative social positions of the participants outside the laboratory (see the experiments of Sampson, 1968, and Lemaine, Lasch and Ricateau, 1971–2), or the congruence of their positions in relation to a social norm for the problem in question (Moscovici, Doise and Dulong,

1972). The significance of these sociological variables, however, may also be studied in a social psychological way. This demonstrates the specific processes which underlie the interactions between individuals in a given social context. In this way, we have been able to study one of the social psychological processes behind group polarization and identify it as being of a cognitive nature.

Our hypothesis was that groups, so as to make interaction between their members possible, emphasise more than individuals certain aspects of the material involved, and that this allows them to agree on clearly defined judgments and thus to reach a position of group polarisation. The question is, what actually happens when a number of individuals, obeying the experimenter's instructions, are required to have a discussion in order to reach a group decision or judgment. Since different aspects of the problem are salient for different individuals, agreement can only be reached after re-definition of the situation. One aspect, or a small number of aspects of the situation must become dominant for all subjects and overrule the various considerations influencing individual responses in different directions. The group therefore has to achieve a real cognitive organisation, whether this is by way of innovation – a new dimension taking priority – or because a form of organisation already accepted by some members of the group comes to be accepted by all. Some experimental situations seem to suggest that the first form of group structuring is especially likely where there are large individual differences (Hall and Watson, 1970; Hall and Williams, 1966). Where individual differences are less, and there is a greater polarisation of individual responses, the second form is more likely. In both cases, our position is that group processes will lead to a form of cognitive structure at least as compelling as that for individual judgments.

The question now is, how this theoretical formulation can be verified. A methodological approach in terms of factor analysis would seem to be indicated. We hypothesise that the first factors deriving from the group responses should show a higher saturation than the first factors deriving from individual responses. The experimental situations must therefore contrast conditions where there is much inter-action among a number of subjects, with conditions in which the subject finds himself alone in coping with given stimulus material. In this way, it should be possible to show that certain kinds of social interaction do indeed have an effect on different forms of cognitive organisation.

The findings of Moscovici, Zavalloni and Weinberger (1972) showing the generality of the phenomenon of group polarisation, provide the basis for a preliminary verification of our hypothesis. Let us briefly recall the purpose of the experiment. Four subjects described five photographs of men in terms of twelve Likert scales. They then had a discussion so as to reach agreement in respect of each scale and each photograph. This experiment provided results confirming the view that the cognitive organisation of group responses is more potent than that of individual responses. The reasoning behind the procedures which we followed in order to verify our hypothesis was as follows. If it is true that groups give more weight to certain significant aspects of the material presented, this should mean that, in a factorial analysis, the first dimension on which the five photographs have loadings should account for a larger part of the variance of the group responses than of the individual responses, on average. This was in fact the case for eight out of ten groups. In respect of the variance accounted for by the first two factors, the groups are superior in nine cases out of ten (Doise, 1973). Our first hypothesis was thus verified, statistically, by the data. Group cognitive struc-turing is more potent than the pre-existing cognitive struc-turing of the individuals who compose the groups. It has further been shown that individuals who, on their own, structure the material more in terms of one main dimension, have more influence in the development of group responses (ibid, p. 138).

The claim to verify a hypothesis on the basis of a re-analysis of the results of an experiment which has already been carried out may be criticised as being based on an 'a posteriori' interpretation. This criticism cannot be brought against the evidence just given, because long before the experiment referred to was carried out, we had already formulated the hypothesis that groups would be more 'unidimensional' than individuals (Doise, 1969a, p. 143). The importance of the hypothesis, however, seemed to call for further confirmation, and accordingly we carried out a study of group interaction in children who had reached the higher levels of concrete operational thinking (10–11 years of age). The experimental material consisted of a series of eight painted cards, based upon three systematically varied criteria. They were orange or blue in colour, triangular or square in shape, and there were two large ones and six small ones. In this experiment, we therefore knew in advance the main characteristics of the material to which the interaction was relevant. The experiment involved an 'individual' condition in which the children, on their own, had to classify the eight cards, first showing which card of the eight, in their opinion, would be best for decorating a classroom. They then had to choose among the remaining seven cards and so on. In a 'group' condition, other children took part in the experiment in groups of three. They were asked to reach agreement on the design which would be best. Otherwise, the 'group' condition was the same as the 'individual' condition.

For the analysis of results an index of the structure of preferences was developed, which took account of the consistency with which the different aspects (colour, shape, height and number) seemed to be important in relation to one another. As predicted, the structuring of group choices was more potent than that for individual choices (Doise, 1973). This experiment therefore confirmed more directly the findings previously referred to. It also extended the range of our hypothesis, by showing its application to groups of children, the members of which had not previously had to make individual decisions.

Children in groups impose a greater degree of structure on concrete material than children on their own. But will a similar difference be found between group structure and individual structure when children are confronted with social material presented to them individually? In order to answer this question, we asked children to give their preferences in respect of different professions. If these preferences are better structured by groups than by individuals, one consequence is inevitable; group choices with regard to different stimuli should be more coherent than the choices made by children working alone with less clearly organised criteria. Specifically, by making subjects choose, by means of the method of paired comparisons, we should find fewer intransitive choices in the group situation than in the individual situation. This prediction was verified as follows. On the basis of clinical interview, five predominantly masculine occupations (baker, male hairdresser, taxi driver, doctor, male teacher) and five predominantly feminine occupations (shop assistant, female hairdresser, secretary, nurse, female teacher) were selected. For each group of occupations, a list of ten possible pairs was drawn up. The masculine group was presented to five groups of three boys who had first, for all the pairs, to indicate their preferences individually and then give their group preferences. The same procedure was followed for five groups of three girls, who used the feminine list. In both the individual session and the group session, subjects had to give the reason for their choice. Two indices were selected for the analysis of results, the number of different criteria put forward to justify the ten choices and the number of intransitive choices made. The latter index consists of the number of intransitive triads – e.g. A is preferred to B, B is preferred to C, but C is preferred to A. Although on average more criteria appear in the group situation (7.6 in the group situation compared with 6.3 in the individual situation), we still find, as predicted, fewer cases of intransitivity in the group situation (M = 0.10) than in the individual situation (M = 0.96). These findings, which are detailed elsewhere (Doise, 1973, p. 143), indicate once again, with different material and a different method, that group cognitive structure is more potent than individual cognitive structure, even though groups have more information to cope with.

The studies outlined were not intended to explain the working of a society. They were neither sociologically oriented nor psychologically oriented. There was no claim to study the effects of social interaction at the individual level. We were simply concerned to show how the dynamics of certain forms of social interaction involved cognitive transformations which might provide the basis for the polarisation which takes place when individuals have to occupy, even provisionally, certain places in the social system. The experiments to which we have referred are examples of social psychological research.

TOWARDS A GENETIC SOCIAL PSYCHOLOGY

Science advances by conceptualising change. In psychology, cognitive development provides a fertile field of change which genetic psychology has fruitfully developed at the theoretical level. At the sociological level, it is economic crises and revolutionary movements, like the recent nationalist and anti-imperialist movements, which stimulate thinking and research. In the social psychological researches previously outlined, the aim was to study a much more limited field of change, such as is involved when one moves from one interaction situation to another in which the interaction is at a higher level. Social psychology turns to the study of various kinds of social interaction in order to conceptualise the differences involved. There seems to us at the present time to be one particularly promising approach, that which consists in trying to integrate individual cognitive development with the development of social interaction.

G. H. Mead has provided a rough conceptualisation of the relations between psychological development and social interaction. Mead insists on the importance of conversation by gesture.

The internalization in our experience of the external conversations of gestures which we carry on with other individuals in the social process is the essence of thinking; and the gestures thus internalized are significant symbols because they have the same meanings for all individual members of the given society or social group, i.e. they respectively arouse the same attitudes in the individuals making them that they arouse in the individuals responding to them: otherwise the individual could not internalize them (Mead, 1934, p. 47).

Repeated reciprocal adjustment of behaviour, especially verbal behaviour, leads to meaning. 'If the individual does himself make use of something answering to the same gesture he observes, saying it over again to himself, putting himself in the role of the person who is speaking to him, then he has the meaning of what he hears, he has the idea: the meaning has become his' (ibid, p. 109). Meaning comes when the individual anticipates the reaction of the other to him. 'Just as in fencing the parry is an interpretation of the thrust, so, in the social act, the adjustive response of one organism to the gesture of another is the interpretation of that gesture by that organism – it is the meaning of that gesture' (ibid, p. 78). The symbol which 'is nothing but the stimulus whose response is given in advance' (ibid, p. 181) makes possible the internalisation of the gesture.

This gives rise to intelligence. 'I know of no way in which intelligence or mind could arise or could have arisen, other than through the internalization by the individual of social processes of experience and behaviour, that is, through this internalization of the conversation of significant gestures, as made possible by the individual's taking the attitudes of other individuals toward himself and toward what is being thought about' (ibid, pp. 191–2).

This bold thesis must be brought into line with that of Piaget concerning the kind of internalised imitation which becomes representation and forms the basis for symbolic thinking. Just as Mead emphasises the role of social interaction in the emergence of meaning, Piaget, as we have seen, agrees that there are close relations between cognitive operations and social interactions. Piaget in fact implies that human intelligence develops in the individual as a function of social interaction. Also, according to Piaget, co-operation between individuals 'is the first of a series of forms of behaviour which are important for the constitution and development of logic' (1950, p. 163).

These two authors therefore give more or less emphasis to the integration of individual and social in their explanations of knowledge. We have tried to show experimentally how this integration works at one level of cognitive development. The general hypothesis behind the experiments which we shall report briefly, is that the co-ordination of actions *between* individuals facilitates the co-ordination of the same actions *by* the individual. When several individuals have to co-ordinate their actions with regard to certain objects, they should be more inclined to co-ordinate their own individual actions with regard to these objects.

We previously showed that children, at a certain stage of development, unable to succeed alone in a well structured cognitive task, did in fact succeed by co-ordinating their actions (Doise, Mugny and Perret-Clermont, 1975). Of course, this kind of support is not sufficient to justify the thesis that social co-operation is necessary for an individual to reach the stage of 'operational thinking'. It represents only a preliminary step. However, any relevant experiment designed to bridge this gap must satisfy certain requirements. In particular, the superior performances in the social situation must not be explicable by laws which assume that a group will succeed when one member of the group is capable of solving the problem. Hence come the two main predictions for confirmation. (1) Two children interacting attain cognitive performance superior to those reached by children faced with the same task by themselves. (2) This superiority differs significantly from the superiority which we would find if one single member sufficed to explain the performance of the pair.

The population of children which we used to confirm our predictions consisted of four classes in a school in the suburbs of Geneva. Sixty boys and girls took part in the experiment, and they came from two classes of average age five years nine months, and two classes of average age six years eight months.

The material, developed after a trial run, was based on the 'Three Mountains' material described by Piaget and Inhelder (1956) in a study of the combining of perspectives in a spatial relations task. It consisted of two games with three 'houses' made up of 'Lego' pieces. Each of the three houses was quite different from the others, and had an opening marking the 'front' of the house. The houses were given names – Ranch (R), small (S), and large (L) house. In one of the games, the experimenter developed a model of a village by assigning each building to specific points on a cardboard base. The other 'three house game' given to the subjects was to construct a copy of the model village on the same base. Every base had the same clearly visible coloured mark as a point of reference for the orientation of the base. The position of this mark varied, and was located towards one corner of the card (Figure 1).

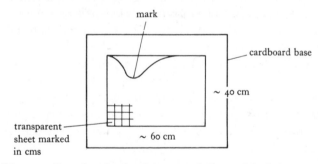

Figure 1. Base for the development of the model of the village and the copy

The subjects stood in front of a table (Figure 2) on which the experimenter set forth the model for each trial. They were asked to reconstruct each village (arranging three houses) on another base on a table placed at an angle of 90 degrees to the left of the subjects. Subjects were told that

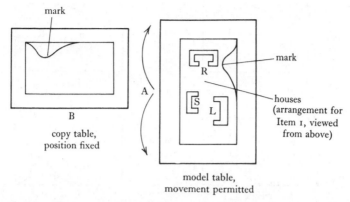

Figure 2. Disposition of subjects at tables with model and copy

they were allowed to go round the models (without touching the material), but that the copy had to be made while they remained at the other table and without turning the base round.

The verbal instructions were given in language suited to children. The experimenter insisted on the example of the man who came out of the lake (the 'mark') and who had to find the houses 'just the same' on the copy as on the model. Since we wanted to compare a situation involving the most spontaneous social interaction possible with a situation as 'individual' as possible, we tried to eliminate as far as possible the direct role of the experimenter. This was limited to ensuring that the experimental procedure was followed. Closed circuit television enabled us to avoid taking records 'on the spot'.

Four tests were devised, two on the basis of the definition of two villages or systems of relations between the houses, the other two by modifying the relation between the two villages and the mark (Figure 3). Each of the model villages was thus presented on a base on which the mark was high and so to the left (as for the copy) or low and to the right (rotation of 180 degrees with respect to the copy, for which the mark was always high and to the left). The four

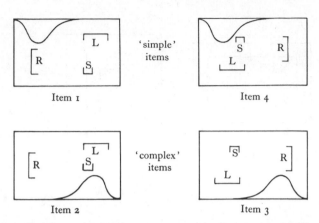

Figure 3. The four models as seen from position A (cf. Figure 2)

test situations obtained in this way (Figure 3) may be divided into 'simple' and 'complex' tests, according to the nature of the transformations the subjects were required to make.

Two experimental conditions were used. In the *individual condition*, the subjects were placed alone in front of the problem and the experimenter had absolutely no communication with the subject. In the *group condition*, the subjects were taken in pairs of the same sex from the same class and were asked to work together and to reach agreement. In both conditions the subjects were asked to tell the experimenter when they thought they had finished their task. For each age level, ten subjects were studied in the individual condition and twenty different subjects in the group condition.

The main experimental measure consisted of the number of houses correctly placed in respect of both localisation and orientation to the opening. The results were added for the two easy tests and for the two difficult tests, the maximum possible index of success being in each case six. Since the age factor was not significant, we give in Table 2a only the means for the factors of experimental condition and test difficulty.

Table 2. (a) *Means of indices of Structure*

Conditions	Simple tests	Complex tests
Individual	4.75	1.30
Collective	5.05	3.30

SOURCE: After Doise, Mugny and Perret-Clermont, 1975

(b) *Results of analysis of variance*

Conditions	Tests	Conditions – tests interaction
$F = 4.358$	$F = 38.886$	$F = 3.438$
d.f. = 1, 36	d.f. = 1, 36	d.f. = 1, 36
$p < 0.05$	$p < 0.001$	$p < 0.10$

An analysis of variance (Table 2b) shows the difference between the two kinds of test to be highly significant. It also confirms the prediction that pairs of subjects would be more successful than subjects alone, especially for the difficult tests. It remains to be confirmed that the effectiveness which results from the social interaction does not represent simply an artefact due to the greater probability that in pairs one of the members may be sufficiently good at the task to be successful independently of his partner. To control for this possible artefact, we found the number of successes to be expected for pairs on the basis of individual successes in the difficult tests. This figure is in fact only three when we count the subjects who have at least *one* complete success. If we now use the formula given by Lorge and Solomon (1955), $p_g = 1 - (1 - p_i)^n$, where p_g is the probability of group success, p_i the probability of individual success and n the number of individuals in a group, we find, according to the hypothesis that if the success of one individual is enough to explain the success of the group, 5.5 pairs should achieve at least one perfect performance in the difficult tests. Now in fact, 14 groups showed such a performance, thus indicating that the group result cannot be attributed to the influence of one individual alone with a superior level of performance. The figure of 14 is significantly higher than the theoretical frequency of 5.5.

This experiment, backed by other similar findings which have been described elsewhere (Doise, Mugny and Perret-Clermont, 1975), shows that social interaction leads in certain conditions to more complex structures than individual action. It has further been confirmed, by means of the same or similar paradigms, that cognitive norms which develop in a social interaction situation are readily accepted by the individual and are likely to be applied again in situations where there is no interaction between pairs (Doise, Mugny and Perret-Clermont, 1975).

The specifically developmental aspect of this approach has been further advanced in other studies. Here, we shall describe three of these (but see also Doise and Mugny, 1975). The first experiment was designed to verify that the superiority of group over individual would also be found in a task consisting of the co-ordination of interdependent motor activities, the subjects being even more strongly encouraged to integrate their actions than in the previous experiment. The primary aim was to show differences in the variations between individual performances and group performances, when the developmental levels studied were varied more widely. If our general hypothesis, to the effect that the development of knowledge proceeds in a specially advantageous way in social situations, is valid, it should be possible to show that a social interaction condition presents cognitive advantages, especially at the genetic stages in the construction of certain operations. A preliminary experiment was therefore carried out to verify the hypothesis that the differences favouring group compared with individual will only be present at a lower developmental level, group performance and individual performance coming together at that level at which it is reasonable to suppose that the co-ordinations involved have been acquired by the subjects individually.

A second question to which we sought an answer concerned the role of verbal communication in the inter-individual exchanges which make group performance superior. A social interaction in which subjects have no chance to communicate verbally should be disturbing compared with a situation in which verbal exchanges are allowed to follow their normal course. One may guess, however, that when co-ordinations of actions are acquired, the absence of verbal communication should have a less disturbing effect upon inter-individual motor co-ordination. In this case, the information provided by observation alone should suffice. On the other hand, the impossibility of verbal exchange should bring back the subjects at the lower level to an individual situation in which each subject would be left to himself and his own centrations, unco-ordinated with those of others. We tried to verify this hypothesis in a second experiment.

A last question concerned the relations between group structure and cognitive performance. The study of the mechanisms involved in the collective regulation of knowledge may be extended to include different group situations. Thus, in a final experiment, concerned with this question, the group structure was manipulated. It was either left to the free choice of the subjects, or imposed in the form of a hierarchy. A hierarchical or centralised group structure may be better adapted to the logical nature of a task and favour its execution (Faucheux and Moscovici, 1960). Our own hypothesis is more complex because it includes reference to a developmental dimension. The 'centralisation' instruction ('one of you is going to be the leader') introduced into the situation a close dependence between the realisation of the goal and the individual qualities of each 'leader'. If the hypothesis of the inferiority of the individual compared with the group is verified at a certain level of development, it seems reasonable to expect that at this level every group situation which makes one member of the group 'special' in

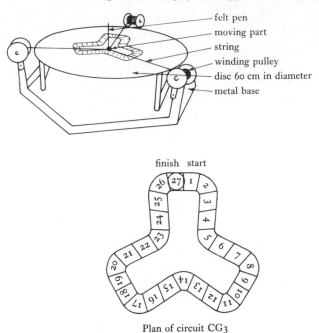

finish　start

Plan of circuit CG3

Figure 4. The co-operative game

relation to others risks lowering appreciably the quality of group performances. In an attempt to answer these three questions, we used a task involving interdependent motor co-ordinations which we called 'the co-operative game', in which subjects had to follow a given path to a moving object attached by strings to pulleys which they manipulated. This task is called co-operative in so far as the performance can only be successful if the joint actions exercised upon the pulleys, which consist of pulling in the string, letting out the string and stopping the string, are the product of a sufficient degree of interaction between the cognitive operations of the different partners in the game. The co-operative game (Figure 4) consists of a disc of 60 cm in diameter, placed at the centre of a metal base surrounded by three vertical posts to which can be attached systems of pulleys to allow the pulling in, letting out or stopping of the string.

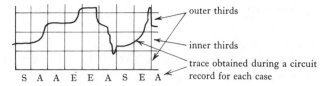

Figure 5. Example of a completed circuit. There is a record,
for each case, of 'success' (S), 'average' (A) or 'error' (E)

The strings were attached to a mobile lead target which
the subjects were able to move. On the disc, there was a card
showing the plan of the path (the breadth corresponding to
the diameter of the moving object) which the subjects had
to follow to the goal. The path naturally differed according
to the number of subjects who had to co-ordinate their
actions. To record the performances of the subject precisely,
a sheet of tracing paper was attached to the card. A felt pen
placed centrally across the perforated target recorded the
precise course of the target. The subjects had to take note
of their performances and accordingly had direct feed-back
about their co-ordination. Finally, the technical arrange-
ment of pulleys allowed three modes of operation; a free run,
a movement from notch to notch and a complete stoppage.
The movement from notch to notch was chosen for all the
experiments described. It offers some resistance to light
pressures which might be due purely to lack of motor
control, while allowing perception of the voluntary pressure
exerted by the other subjects. Moreover, in the individual
condition, this position avoids the motor difficulties or difficulties of laterality which one finds in susbjects not used to
this kind of task.

To calculate performance scores, the path was divided
breadth-wise into three equal thirds (Figure 5). For the
three-person game, 27 trials had to be handled by the scorer.
The trial was considered to be successful (S) when the
recorded trace fell wholly within the middle third. If the
record encroached on either of the outside thirds, or fell
wholly within these limits, the performance was regarded

as average (A). And finally, cases in which the record encroached upon the surface outside the path or fell wholly in this area, were classified as 'error' (E). In the case of the two-person game, the area to be covered by the subjects was less, and two symmetrical paths of the same kind were used (Figure 6). Here, each path was numbered from 1 to 13. To calculate the performance score, the path was this time divided in respect of length, into 88 units each of about 4 mm; the use of more divisions meant that the measure was increased in precision. In all the experiments reported, the score was always obtained by subtracting the number of 'E' cases from the number of 'S' cases.

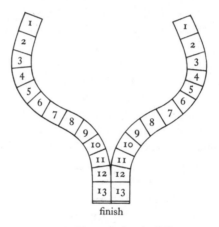

Figure 6. Plan of circuit CG2

The two-person group game provided verification for the superiority of the group, but only at certain developmental levels. In this experiment, the subjects were placed in front of the apparatus, individually or in pairs. In the individual condition, the child was told to carry out a first run by means of two pulleys, and then a second run. The pairs were asked to follow the same paths and in the same orders as the individuals, but here each subject was operating a pulley. The subjects were told that they could talk to one another. The children, of whom one half were aged between 7 and

8 years (level 1) and the other half between 9 and 10 years (level 2), formed pairs which were taken, in each case, from two different classes. Forty-eight subjects altogether were involved of whom eight were in each of the individual conditions 1 and 2, and 16 in the social conditions 1 and 2.

Table 3. *Mean index of performance of individuals and groups of different age levels*

	Level 1 (7–8 years)	Level 2 (9–10 years)
Individual condition	46	54
Group condition	59	59

The index was found by subtracting the number of 'E' cases from the number of 'S' cases. The index refers to the better performance of the two circuits. Number of measures for each case = 8. Difference between the two conditions for level 1: $p < 0.04$ (Mann–Whitney U-test).

Table 3 gives the means of the best performances achieved by individuals and by pairs. The difference between individuals and pairs is significant at the lower level, but not at the higher level. The results show, therefore, that the group is superior to individuals, but only at a certain age level, since this superiority becomes less marked as development proceeds. This suggests once more that cognitive operations are primarily acquired through social interaction and are only later elaborated individually.

If groups do better than individuals on this task, but only at a certain level of development, might it perhaps be possible to suggest the hypothesis advanced by Smedslund (1966), that such superiority is due to an exchange and eventually a conflict of communication? Once the necessary operations are acquired, communication is no longer essential for carrying out the task in question and so the lack of verbal communication would cause disturbance only at the lower level and not at the higher level.

A second experiment with the co-operative game was

intended to verify this prediction. In a 'speaking' condition, the subjects, three in a group, received the same instructions as the subjects in the previous experiment; permission to speak was defined in the same way. In the 'silent' condition, subjects were asked to avoid any kind of verbal communication. Even if one allows for non-verbal communication (head movements, winking or gesture), it is clear that in this condition, subjects are, to a certain extent, deprived of feed-back from others, although by action they can express particular expectations concerning others' actions, just as expressions of irritation can indicate disagreement. Subjects of about 7 years of age (level 1), of about 8 years of age (level 2) and of about 10 years of age (level 3), all pupils of the same Genevan school took part in the experiment. In all, there were 72 subjects, divided into four groups of three for each of the three 'speaking' conditions, and for each of the three 'silent' conditions.

Table 4. *Mean index of performance of 'speaking' and 'silent' groups at different age-levels*

	Level 1 (7 years)	Level 2 (8 years)	Level 3 (10 years)
'Speaking' condition	−1	8	8.75
'Silent' condition	−10	−1.25	7

The index is found by subtracting the number of 'E' cases from the number of 'S' cases. The index refers to the single circuit. Number of measures for each case = 4. Difference between conditions for levels 1 and 2: $p < 0.03$ (Mann–Whitney U-test).

The results presented in Table 4 are in agreement with the hypotheses. For the lower levels (condition 1 and 2 combined) there is a significant difference between the spontaneous and silent interaction conditions, but this difference no longer appears with subjects of ten years of age. The genetic contribution of the group to the individual, shown in the preceding experiments, is here reflected in a kind of

superiority comparable to that of the spontaneous interaction group over the restricted interaction group, at certain
levels of development.

The imposing of a leader of their own age upon subjects
between seven and eight years of age, who have not yet
mastered individually the cognitive operations involved in
the game, and who have, as we have confirmed, a highly
unidirectional view of authority, should have the effect of
disturbing their interaction. This kind of disturbance should
no longer appear, or should be less important, in more
advanced subjects who have more mastery of the necessary
operations and who see more reciprocity in the authority
relationship. Our third experiment was designed to verify
this prediction.

The experimental groups in the social conditions of the
first experiment constitute the control groups for this experiment. In this condition, the subjects were in groups of
two. The other half of the subjects were put in a group
hierarchical condition, the instructions requiring one of
these subjects to play the role of leader for the first trial, the
other subject being leader for the second trial. To ensure
that the subjects followed the instructions as closely as
possible, the group was first asked what a leader was. The
subjects in the hierarchical groups were of the same age
and came from the same school as those constituting the
spontaneous interaction control groups in this experiment.

The results, based on figures derived by subtracting the
number of errors from the number of successes, and given
in Table 5, fully confirm the predictions. In fact, while
subjects at both levels are equally successful in the spontaneous social condition, the subjects in the hierarchical
condition at the lower age are at a serious disadvantage, since
their mean performance is even lower than that of the
children on their own in the first experiment. This effect is
reversed in the case of the older subjects. Perhaps the
designation of 'leader' may, in certain groups, enable the
most efficient subject to raise the score of the group.

It seems to us defensible to conclude on the basis of our

Table 5. *Mean index of performance of 'spontaneous' and 'hierarchical' groups at different age levels*

	Level 1 (7–8 years)	Level 2 (9–10 years)
'Spontaneous' condition	59	59
'Hierarchical' condition	43	71

The index is found by subtracting the number of 'E' cases from the number of 'S' cases. The index refers to the better performance of the two circuits.

Difference between the two conditions:
at level 1: $p < 0.05$
at level 2: $p < 0.10$

Difference between the two levels for the hierarchical condition: $p < 0.02$ (Mann–Whitney U-test).

first studies in genetic social psychology that this approach should provide a fruitful way of integrating the two levels of psychology and sociology. On the one hand, these studies show how social factors predispose the individual, while at the same time indicating how unjustifiable it is to hasten into social psychological generalisations. Each of the factors with which we are concerned, the individual factor and the sociological factor, reflects its own particular form of development. Thus, the social competence of the individual changes during his development. But there is also a problem of generality when one approaches social psychology from the point of view of sociology. We shall now turn to this issue.

PROBLEMS OF GENERALITY AND VALIDITY

Students estimate the apparent movement of a point of light in a blacked-out laboratory, children reconstruct the model of a village or make a design alone, or in pairs or threes. These experiments, which we have reported above, are concerned with very special situations and involve very special groups of subjects. Can they in fact provide a basis for theoretical constructs with some degree of validity and generality? The second part of the present book answers this question in the affirmative by showing how experiments of this kind have laid the foundation for an intergroup social psychology which can accommodate a very wide range of phenomena.

We must correct some misunderstandings. Social psychological experimentation always takes place in a well-determined social context, at a particular moment in the history of a given society. By introducing changes, admittedly limited and conditional, but in different directions, experiment can throw light on the workings of the relations between individuals and groups. Consider, for example, the images which the groups in a society come to have of each other. Hypotheses can be advanced concerning the role of these images in the maintenance of the prevailing relations between these groups. Experimentation, by strengthening or weakening, even temporarily, the customary relations between the members of different groups, can confirm whether the changes induced in the images are compatible with the hypotheses concerning their role. A better understanding of the social psychological aspects of the functioning of a society may thus result from experiment.

Is the sole object of social psychological study the understanding of the ways in which individuals participate in a limited situation in space and time? Relevant to this question, Gergen (1973) has written to the effect that the very process of demonstrating social psychological laws, *ipso facto* creates the historical conditions to invalidate these laws; man will reject the social psychological dynamics of which he is aware. We shall not insist on the similarity – dangerous for the author – between such a statement and the enunciation of a law which has been subject to experimental investigation in the form of 'psychological reactance' (Brehm, 1966). We would in fact rather not use the term 'social psychological law', which seems to imply too readily the existence of regularities observable at the behavioural level. It would be futile to try to find outside the laboratory forms of behaviour induced in highly specific situations. Social psychological experiment is not intended to duplicate, to reproduce on a small scale, or to sample situations outside the laboratory. No doubt the aim of comparable activities is frequently to predict as closely as possible the appearance of forms of behaviour (voting, consumer behaviour, opinions) in a well-structured context. Such is not the purpose of social psychological experiment as we conceive it.

In fact, we think of it as contributing to a level of explanation which is both at a more elementary and at a more general level. Although the kinds of behaviour by which individuals come to be involved in the web of society may differ and vary according to past psychological and sociological development, in view of our position that the psychological and sociological can be integrated, our basic hypothesis remains that stable elementary processes play a part in influencing these behaviours. There is no reason to suppose that such processes occur for the first time in contemporary society. Although we claim a certain generality for social psychological studies it is not on the basis of a universal human nature. The universality of human nature has too often been the basis of ideological argument in defence of values which themselves reflect particular kinds of social relations.

However, although 'human nature' as it appears may be very variable and subject to conditioning, it is still possible that the different forms which human nature assumes may result from different combinations of simple, elementary processes.

The present task of social psychological experiment is to create situations appropriate to isolating these processes and studying the way in which they operate. It should thus become possible to examine how these various processes interact to produce such complex and varied results. Such a task cannot be carried out in a social vacuum. Experimental subjects are also citizens. They bring into the experimental situation a whole body of ideas, norms and representations which in fact constitute the raw material of which the experimenter must study the transformations. General processes manifest themselves in such transformations.

Psychology and sociology develop independently while providing one another with instruments of research. They also provide analogies and isomorphisms. At the present level, we are concerned with general theoretical points of view. Empirical investigation provides us with more detail about how the collective develops by social interaction and correspondingly, how individual development may result from such interaction. Like actions, representations are constantly combining and changing in the course of the development of social relations. They assume importance and combine with one another in accordance with the reciprocal positions occupied by the social actors. Our aim is to find stable basic processes which will be relevant across such changes. The remaining part of this book will be devoted to a more detailed study of the kind of process which takes place when individuals, belonging to different social categories, interact.

PART II

Intergroup relations and category differentiation

Neither psychology nor sociology provides an adequate basis for the study of intergroup relations. A social psychological approach such as we have outlined in Part I is needed to complement these established approaches. In the rest of this book we shall consider the social psychology of intergroup relations, limiting ourselves, however, to the experimental exploration of the field.

At first sight, the experimental study of groups may appear futile. Intergroup relations develop, perhaps more than any other form of social interaction, in a historical context. We have no tools for intervening experimentally at the historical level. We simply cannot study experimentally the 'natural divisions' described by Moscovici (1968), nor the changes in the relations of production within a society. But the problem can be regarded otherwise when the object of study becomes the way in which individual and social are integrated in intergroup relations. With this end in view, we may study at the individual level, the operation of norms, representations and actions, which reflect the expression at the individual level, of more general group processes, and may relate this kind of function to situations involving relations which have been experimentally produced. Thus it is possible to study how, in different conditions, individuals may modify norms, representations and behaviour, while in turn being themselves modified by this process. There is therefore a point, both theoretical and empirical, at which intergroup experimentation may usefully be employed.

A 'constructivist' conception, analogous to that proposed

by Holzkamp (1972), underlies the experimental study of intergroup relations. This conception views science as proceeding basically by creating situations essentially structured in a way analogous to the 'real' situation which one wants to study but also supposes that the 'real', through the transformations which we impose upon it, may end by reproducing the structures produced experimentally. However, in the social psychology of intergroup relations, it is impossible to create situations which have all the characteristics of the complex dynamic reality. The experimental problem is to isolate conceptually certain aspects of the total process and to reproduce these under as controlled conditions as possible, so as to verify whether the results reflect the existing constructs. In the case of intergroup relations, this involves the definition of important aspects of intergroup dynamics, the isolation of typical behaviour, norms and representations and the re-creation of situations in which these factors reappear and can be varied systematically. What happens in an experimental intergroup situation will validate or invalidate the model which has been advanced to explain the relevant intergroup dynamics. Experiment should therefore indicate how far social phenomena can be constructed and modified according to given models. A certain degree of artificiality is inevitably involved in the experimental creation of intergroup situations. The aim of experiment might be regarded in fact as the isolation of one of these processes, the complex interaction of which constitutes historical development.

The first chapter of this part of the book will be concerned with developing more general theoretical and experimental approaches to intergroup relations. The experiments which we shall present, while they do not really penetrate to the level of social psychological processes, nevertheless show that intergroup experimentation is possible. One may think of the experiments described as bearing on the primary material, which is then transformed by the process of category differentiation, as described, with appropriate experimental illustrations, in the penultimate chapter.

I

Experiments on intergroup relations

The experiments to which we shall refer in this chapter represent a close approximation in miniature to certain kinds of real-life situations involving intergroup relations. Indeed, the first studies of which we shall take account, those of Sherif, were carried out in a real-life setting. These studies stimulated the development of a body of theory, the general drift and limitations of which we shall describe. Although Sherif's theory accounts for quite a body of findings, it does not adequately cover all cases. In particular, the dynamics specific to the representations which appear in intergroup interaction require a more appropriate analysis, which we shall attempt to provide at the end of the present chapter.

SHERIF'S EXPLORATORY EXPERIMENTS

The historical and theoretical importance of the researches by Sherif and his collaborators (1961) on group interaction is unquestionable. In fact, not only was Sherif the first to undertake experimental research in this field; he also developed a body of theory concerning competition and co-operation between groups.

We shall describe here only the procedure and results of the most exhaustive of his studies of intergroup processes, that known by the name of the *Robbers' Cave* experiment. Two groups of children of about twelve years of age, all psychologically well adjusted, were involved in pleasurable activities which required active participation from each child. They camped in the woods, cooked their meals, decided upon a place to bathe in the river and transported their boats across a strip of rough country. During this phase of group formation, the two groups had no knowledge of one another. For both groups, as predicted, participation in attractive activities had the effect of creating a real group structure. Norms developed, one group particularly emphasising toughness (swearing, and refusal to bother about injuries, for example), while the other group took a milder outlook (its members prayed before their tasks). As indicated by sociometric measures, there was a hierarchy of social ranks and roles. After a few days, the two groups each showed a stable hierarchical structure.

Once the two groups were properly formed, they were brought into contact. At this point, the experimenters, who were the directors of the camp, organised a contest. The two groups opposed one another in pleasurable but competitive games – treasure hunt, tug-of-war, games of baseball and football, competition in putting up a tent, etc. During this competitive phase, strong hostility developed; on the very first day of the contest, the group which lost captured the victors' flag and burned it. During the following days, there were raids on each side to disrupt the sleeping quarters of the other group. Continual oaths were exchanged. Appropriate measures, obtained informally, indicated that competition strongly influenced the perceptions, representations and attitudes of the antagonists. Thus, the image of the out-group became very unfavourable compared with the image of the in-group. The performance of team-mates was overestimated compared with others. The structure of the groups also changed. Solidarity increased, and, for one of the groups, the social hierarchy changed in that the 'leader' was replaced by another member who was more active in the struggle with the opposing group.

How then could this conflict be ended? If competition, i.e. incompatibility of aims of the two groups led to hostility, perhaps a reconciliation of aims might bring a reconciliation of groups. The response was negative. Two groups can well pursue similar and compatible goals without any reduction of mutual hostility. Sherif takes note of this in the third phase of his experiment, in which the groups were brought into contact without being interdependent. During this phase, non-competitive activities such as eating together, going together to a film show or a fireworks show, did nothing to reduce the hostility between the groups.

Relaxation of hostility came about only when the two groups had to make several attempts, in co-operation, to resolve problems of concern to all. This took place during the fourth phase of the experiment, in which the groups were confronted with superordinate goals. Such a goal is, by definition, extremely important for both groups, and the obstacles in the way are such that they cannot be overcome by one group alone. Thus, the groups had to trace the source of a leak in the water supply, pay an exaggerated price to hire a film, and repair the van which was bringing them supplies. The effect of co-operation was not immediate. Only after the pursuit of several superordinate goals did the intergroup hostility begin to abate. The image of the other group became almost as favourable as that of the membership group, and the choice of best friends began to be made across the borders between the two groups.

Let us summarise the findings of this experiment in terms of the theoretical formulation proposed by Sherif (1951) long before this experiment was carried out. Individuals seeking to attain an end by interdependent action become a group and develop a social hierarchy and specific norms. When two groups are set to realise incompatible ends, and one group cannot attain its goal unless the other fails to do so, an unfavourable perception develops between the groups and the members of the one group can only think of and realise hostile contacts with the members of the other group. They increase the solidarity within their own group while, of necessity, adjusting their social structure to the conflict situation. The only thing which can reduce this hostility is the realisation of superordinate goals which require a common effort on the part of all the members of both groups. This has the effect of making the perception of the other group more favourable, and permits the establishment of comradeship among the members of the two groups. According to Sherif, then, studying the relations of the goals of different interacting groups should lead to an understanding of the social psychological phenomena involved in intergroup relations.

GENERALITY OF THE EFFECTS OF COMPETITION

To appreciate fully the implications of the results and the range of the ideas put forward by Sherif, we should first recall some studies which have contributed to verifying the generality of Sherif's results, especially with regard to competition. This form of group interaction has been the subject of many studies. One of the first studies, which we shall describe here, was carried out by Blake and Mouton (1962b) on 'training' groups composed of adults, executives in industrial organisations and in medical and research institutes. All 48 groups studied consisted of eight to ten members. In each case, a competition was arranged between two, three or four of these groups as follows. During the first ten or twelve hours, each group worked on its own so that a group structure might develop. After this group formation phase, each group had to consider for three hours a problem in human relations which was equally familiar to all the groups concerned. The experimenter announced in advance that a winning group and a losing group would be nominated, the possibility of a tie being excluded. After the groups had provided their solutions, these were reproduced and distributed to all the members of the groups involved. They were asked to judge them in terms of quantity and relevance. Out of 48 groups studied, the solution of the membership group was judged superior to the solutions of other groups in 46 groups, while the members of the two remaining groups gave the same average score to the solution of their own group and that of other groups.

The significance of this experiment is that, unlike most

experiments in social psychology, it used adults who were not students as subjects. Another study which used adult subjects was that of Bass and Dunteman (1963). They were concerned with the distortion of judgments of an allied group in a win-or-lose situation. During a stage of sensitisation to group phenomena, eight or nine groups of managers had each to co-operate with another group in an attempt to find a solution to a problem involving judgment of a social situation, better than those proposed by two other groups concerned. A judge was selected from each group to judge the output of the different groups without knowing from which group they came. The task occupied a whole day, and the subjects were required to describe their own group and the other groups at different points in the experiment. They did this before the division into allies and opponents, again when competition was instituted, a third time after the 'neutral' judges had given their results, and finally the morning after the end of the experiment. The results show that in general, allied groups and opposing groups were judged less favourably than membership groups. However, the fact that a group becomes a co-operative group increases its evaluated status. Immediately after the announcement of results, the inferior groups lower the scores which they attribute to themselves and so come to give themselves the same scores as they give to the opposing groups. But the scores which they award themselves tend to increase later. The overvaluation of one's own group is temporarily upset when it comes into conflict with reality, but the effect of announcing a poor achievement makes itself particularly felt in the description of the allied group which is even more poorly judged. The authors actually associate their findings with the mistaken judgment behind the incident of the Bay of Pigs. The Americans overvalued the power of their allies and undervalued the power of their adversaries.

Diab's (1970) work returns to Sherif's 'model' of the experimental method, although it was conducted in a different cultural context, and there may have been some distortion owing to the transposition of an experimental situation from one society to another. In social psychology as we conceive it, a procedure which reveals a particular social psychological process in one culture does not necessarily imply the existence of a similar process in a different culture. Other variables may play a more important part than those manipulated by the experimenter and introduce too much 'noise' in the experimental design. Diab's (1970) experiment was as follows.

The subjects were pupils of schools in Beirut in the Lebanon. They were of 11 years of age, were unacquainted with one another; half were Christians and half Moslems. As in Sherif's experiment (1951), all the subjects began by taking part in common activities and, after several days, were divided into two groups. This division was made in such a way that sociometric choices, religious affiliation and athletic ability were distributed equally between the two groups. The two groups were allowed four days in which to organise themselves and were then made to compete. A further stage of the experiment which should have introduced contacts, the intervention of adults condemning aggression, and superordinate projects, had to be abandoned because the experimenters were unable to control the aggression of some of the children.

The results duplicate Sherif's findings in many ways. Those who participate in pleasurable communal activities form a social structure. During the competitive stage, each group tends to see itself in a more favourable light, although this tendency is not statistically significant. The victorious group may judge its performance as better than that of the other group, but the losing group does not. Both groups showed the development of a hierarchy in the group. No data could be collected for the fourth stage. Four members of the losing group wanted to leave the camp; they had developed a high degree of aggressiveness with regard both to the winning group, and to one member of the losing group.

An appeal to differences in cultural context does not seem adequate to explain the rather different results obtained by Sherif and Diab. Even in the second stage of the experiment, the sociometric choices and rejections were less based on group demarcation in the Lebanese experiment. This may perhaps be explained, especially in the light of results we ourselves obtained in an experiment on conflicting group loyalties (Deschamps and Doise, 1974), by the fact that each group was composed of children from two religious affiliations. It therefore seems not to be pure chance that the four children who wanted to leave the camp and their group, were of the same religion. Again, from the beginning, the structure of the groups was particularly authoritarian, although there was a distinct difference between the two groups. At the competition stage, the group with the more authoritarian structure actually lost. There are therefore several possible explanations of the apparently equivocal behaviour of group members with respect to their membership group. The different findings of Diab's experiment are not, therefore, necessarily to be accounted for in cultural terms. Bass and Dunteman have already confirmed that relative overvaluation does not always occur. We shall later show that the impossibility of a group attaining its goal contributes toward its disintegration.

As far as competition is concerned, Sherif's hypotheses seem to have fairly general significance. Sherif's theory can also be followed up in another way; it provides an explanation of limiting cases in intergroup relations.

THE FUSION AND FISSION OF GROUPS

The introduction of a series of superordinate goals reduces or eliminates the conflict and the related social psychological effects. Thus at the end of Sherif's experiment the views that the groups held of one another tended to overlap. Were there then still two groups in the Robber's Cave? Without questioning Sherif's position, this is a reasonable issue to raise.

According to Sherif, and as was shown in the first stage of the experiment described, individuals who, in a situation involving interdependence, seek to achieve goals which are attractive to all, come to form a group. But how does the earlier stage of Sherif's experiment differ from the latter stage? At both stages, activities covering the whole psychological field integrated the actions of all concerned. According to Sherif's own assumptions, each stage should involve the emergence of a group.

The question is whether the group emerging at the end of the experiment could have developed without the combining of the two pre-existing groups. Sherif's position offers no answer to this question. His results seem to imply that the frontiers between groups tend to disappear, since sociometric choices, another criterion in terms of which Sherif delimits his groups, come to depend less on membership of one of the two groups.

By the end of the experiment, the basic aims of the two groups had become the same. This represents a limiting case in intergroup relations, since the separate groups tended to disappear as separate entities.

It is possible for circumstances to undermine a group goal, or prevent its achievement. This was the case in French's study (1941). His experiment was intended to demonstrate differences between two kinds of groups – organised and unorganised – in a situation involving frustration and fear. Frustration was introduced by requiring the groups to solve insoluble intellectual or manual problems. The organised groups were drawn from sports teams or youth clubs. The unorganised groups were composed of students who were unacquainted with one another. On the whole, concern and mutual verbal aggression were more common in the organised groups. These groups, however, did not disintegrate while in half of the unorganised groups, some individuals dissociated themselves from the others to work alone. French explains the greater aggression in the organised groups by the fact that these groups were more cohesive, allowed greater freedom within the group, were also more used to striving together, and were thus more affected by their inability to achieve the goals set, and more ready to talk about it. The greater internal cohesiveness of these groups meant that they could avoid disintegration. In the groups in which the members had not been previously associated, there was less pressure, but even less cohesiveness. Differences concerning ways of reaching the goal were enough to create dissidence. We shall not concern ourselves with the methodological problems raised by this well-known experiment. A number of significant variables were not controlled for. In terms of interpretation, however, it seems to us possible to reformulate French's conclusions by taking up the notion of goal or end. For the organised groups, the experimental goal was only peripheral to the main goal justifying the existence and continuation of the group. For the unorganised groups, the only goal involved was the accomplishment of the experimental task. The impossibility of attaining this goal deprived the group of its grounds for justification. Ethnological observations support this interpretation. Chance (1962), commenting on Beals (1962), shows how, in a Hindu society, the goals of a village group in contact with Western culture had become modified, while traditional culture had failed to change in such a way as to satisfy these goals. This situation gave rise to deviant, conflicting and disruptive behaviour which persisted until the village took over from urban culture the means of attaining its new aspirations.

When it is impossible for a group to attain its goal, we find schism and division. This represents another limiting case, where a group is transformed into new groups, and can readily be interpreted in Sherif's terms. Indeed, in one of his first experiments on intergroup relations, did not Sherif form his two experimental groups from a single initial group? The division which he created was induced by preventing the members of one camp from continuing their participation in the same attractive activities as the others; and this in effect meant that they could not realise common ends.

THE DISCRIMINATIVE EFFECT, OR SOCIAL COMPETITION

One of the main characteristics of competitive interaction between groups is its discriminative effect, as shown in the form of accentuation of differences between the groups at the perceptual, affective and behavioural levels. The question is whether this discrimination is due entirely to the incompatibility of goals, or whether a more general phenomenon is involved. The experiments reported below provide arguments in favour of a general interpretation.

In an investigation of the factors leading to overvaluation of the product of one's own group, Ferguson and Kelley (1964) found that the factors involved did not consist exclusively in competition for material gain or in contribution to the output of the product. They asked the members of their experimental groups to work efficiently and constructively at various tasks (making a toy, designing an urban plan and making up a modern fairy story). No actual competition between groups was created. After the completion of each task, a member who had been unable to take part in carrying it out, had to judge its worth. The production of his own group was overvalued in relation to that of the other group, both when he was able to take part in the process involved, and when he was not. In the latter case, however, no clear justification was available for the limits and shortcomings of one's own group.

Rabbie and Horwitz (1969) report a similar evaluative discrimination, which involves the perception of persons and groups with whom the subjects do or do not share the same fate. In this experiment, eight persons, who were unacquainted with one another, came to the laboratory and were divided, ostensibly for administrative reasons, into a 'blue' group and a 'green' group. The experiment was presented to them as having to do with the development of first impressions of other people. The subjects were divided into two groups. First of all, individually, they took a test and a questionnaire and described two photographs. Then, the experimenter told the subjects that the reward for taking part in the experiment unfortunately consisted of only four transistors, which would be given to the members of one group according to the experimental conditions, by chance, according to the experimenter's decision or by a vote by all eight subjects in the experiment. One of the groups then did indeed receive the four transistors. In the control condition, the experimenter said nothing at all about reward. Then the subjects came along and briefly gave their 'first' impressions of all the participants, using the same scales as they had used to describe the photographs. They were also asked to describe the general characteristics of the two groups. There was no difference between the descriptions of their own group and those of the other group in the control situation (no reward), but these differences were significant in the experimental groups. Both those who were rewarded and those who were frustrated, in general described the members and the characteristics of their own group more favourably than the members and atmosphere of the other group. The mere fact of sharing a common fate, regardless of its origin, thus seems to be sufficient to induce evaluative discrimination in favour of one's membership group.

Competitive interaction is not essential for the emergence of either perceptual and evaluative discrimination or affective discrimination. It is sufficient, as Sherif *et al.* (1961) show, for individuals no longer to be able to take part in the same activities, for their friendship ties to be restructured so as to enable them to belong to a group which engages in common activities.

Representations and affect reflect the boundaries between groups. Behaviour seems to reflect these boundaries to an even greater degree. Using young French and German subjects, in a mixed motivation situation, we ran a series of trials in which two pairs of young people, of the same nationality (homogeneous groups), or a French pair with a German pair (heterogeneous groups), or two pairs each composed of a Frenchman and a German (mixed groups) engaged in interaction. As in a procedure previously used by Wilson, Chun and Kayatani (1965), two kinds of decision had to be made; first in respect of the other pair and then in respect of one's partner in the same pair. The experimental rules in respect of decisions between pairs were as follows. When two pairs both chose red (by putting a red token under a cover), each group was awarded two points. When both pairs chose blue, they were awarded no points. When one pair decided in favour of blue and the other in favour of red, the blue pair were given four points and the red pair no points. After each decision between pairs, and before they knew the choice of the other pair, the two partners of each pair tried again between themselves to determine how to share the profit. Twenty intergroup decisions and twenty inter-partner decisions had to be made. Table 6 indicates that the number of co-operative choices was always greater between partners than between pairs, especially when the groups were heterogeneous. This was in fact the only condition in which the difference in group membership of the experimental pairs was determined by a difference in nationality.

Table 6. *Differences between the mean number of co-operative choices within and between pairs*

Heterogeneous groups	Mixed groups	Homogeneous groups
5.23	2.25	2.30

This index shows that co-operative choices are always more frequent within pairs than between pairs, especially when temporary membership of interest groups coincides with membership of different previous groups.

SOURCE: after Doise, 1969d.

Tajfel and his colleagues (Tajfel, 1970; Tajfel, Billig, Bundy and Flament, 1971) attempted to investigate the minimum conditions necessary to induce discriminatory behaviour between groups. The subjects in their experiment were pupils in the same school, who knew each other well. They began the experiment with a task involving visual perception or aesthetic judgment. Then, they were told that they were going to be divided into two groups, according to the results of the preceding task, either into a group of 'over-estimators' and a group of 'under-estimators', or into a 'Klee' group and a 'Kandinsky' group. The subjects were led to believe that this division was made on the basis of their performance on the initial task. In fact, it was done on a chance basis. Each subject was told to which group he had been assigned. No-one knew to which group his various comrades belonged. The next part of the experiment involved decision making. With the help of several tables, subjects decided what reward their comrades should receive for taking part in the experiment. Each table had to do with the rewards to be given to two pupils. These two pupils might belong to the same group or to different groups. The subjects never knew to which friend the rewards would go. They knew only the group membership and code number of those to whom they were assigning the reward. They never rewarded themselves.

Table 7. *Examples of matrices used by Tajfel*

						Matrix 'a'							
5	6	7	8	9	10	11	12	13	14	15	16	17	18
18	17	16	15	14	13	12	11	10	9	8	7	6	5
						Matrix 'b'							
7	8	9	10	11	12	13	14	15	16	17	18	19	
1	3	5	7	9	11	13	15	17	19	21	23	25	

For each matrix, subjects are told to which category the individual who will receive the values *above* belongs, and to which category the individual who will receive the values *below* belongs. They choose one case per matrix to indicate the rewards for the individuals concerned.

SOURCE: Tajfel, 1970.

In Table 7, we give two examples of the tables actually used. The numbers represent tenths of a penny. The same

table can be used several times; the upper and lower numbers are assigned either to two persons belonging to the same
group, or to two persons belonging to the two different
groups, the upper numbers being assigned to members of
one group, the lower numbers being assigned to members
of the other group. In every case, subjects had to select a
single column in each table. It can be seen that in the case
of matrix 'a', the central cases represent fair reward; in the
case of matrix 'b', the extreme right cases benefit everyone.

If subjects have to reward two pupils from the same group,
using matrix 'a', they use the middle section of the matrix.
On the other hand, when they have to make a decision in
respect of a member of their own group and a member
of the other group, the subjects abandon 'fair play' by
consistently favouring their in-group member compared
with the other person. In the case of type 'b' matrices, the
numbers toward the right end of the matrix are chosen only
when it is a question of rewarding two members of one's own
group. On the other hand, when only the values on the top
are given to a member of one's own group, the values to the
left are more frequently chosen. Subjects thus consistently
favoured the members of their own group, when they could,
to the disadvantage of the others (matrix 'a'); but reduced
their group's gain in absolute terms in order to avoid a
situation in which their partners, while receiving more in
absolute terms, got less than the others (matrix 'b').

Tajfel (1972) has developed a theoretical framework to
take account of these findings. He advances a more 'social'
version of Festinger's social comparison theory (1954).
According to Festinger, individuals evaluate their opinions
and abilities by comparing them with those of other individuals. According to Tajfel, self-evaluation is based on the
social identity which the individual acquires as a result of
his membership of various groups. Belonging to a group
contributes to the development of a positive social identity
if this group can be favourably compared with other groups.
'A social group will maintain its contribution to those aspects
of the social identity of an individual which are positively

valued by this individual, only if the group in question can maintain such positive valuations as distinct from those of other groups' (Tajfel, 1972, p. 296). Individuals actively attempt to establish a positively evaluated difference between their own group and other groups. Thus in the experiment reported, the subjects established a positive difference between their own group and the other group, even though in order to do so they had to reduce their own monetary gains in absolute terms. They were ready to pay a price to gain a positive social identity.

Turner (1975) develops Tajfel's ideas by proposing the notion of 'social competition'. By this, he means the kind of competition which groups use in their attempts to establish a positive difference among them. Turner's approach differs from Sherif's in that, whereas Sherif explains both competition and co-operation between groups, Turner takes account only of a unilateral tendency in a group to establish a positive difference from another group. The possibility of a superordinate goal is therefore not envisaged by the exponents of 'positive social identity'.

The notion of social competition provides the basis for an experiment by Turner (1972) relating to the conditions under which division into two groups does not inevitably lead to discrimination. The underlying idea of this experiment was that subjects who felt no need to discriminate between groups in order to achieve a positive identity would not discriminate between members of their own group and members of another group. The subjects had to use the matrices of Tajfel et al. (1971) to decide upon the rewards they themselves should receive, and those which others should receive. The 'others', who consisted of the subjects' membership group and members of the other group were therefore, in this experiment, opposed to the 'self' of each subject. There could therefore be competition between self and other, which was not possible in Tajfel's experiments, and competition in terms of membership of the two groups. Results clearly showed that competition between self and other might be more important than competition between

groups. Turner (1975, p. 19n) draws the following conclusion.

Subjects will identify with a social category to the extent that such
identification enables them to achieve value significance, to the
extent that it is the category most relevant to the desire for
positive self-evaluation in the experimental situation. Thus, it can
be said that in the experiment by Tajfel et al. it was not the
division into groups which caused discrimination but rather that the
group dichotomy was the only existing categorization through
which a more basic motivation might be expressed.

By carrying Tajfel's ideas to their logical conclusion, Turner
thus manages to create another limiting situation, in which
intergroup relations give place to inter-individual relations.
In our concluding chapter, we shall see that intergroup
interaction has, however, certain qualities which distinguish
it from interaction among individuals.

INTERGROUP RELATIONS AND GROUP STRUCTURE

Group solidarity increases during competitive interaction,
and either becomes more clearly defined or is adapted to
circumstances. Sherif noted this in his experiments, and
there are many 'natural' observations which confirm it. But
again, competition for an objective and immediate reward
does not seem to be essential for the occurrence of such
phenomena. The mere presence, actual or symbolic, of a
rival or hostile group is enough.

Within a given group, there appears to be a connection
between the overestimation of the other's performance and
the social position occupied by this other among the members of the group. Harvey (1956) assumed that this connection became stronger when a social structure became more
salient, and proposed the hypothesis that such an increase
would appear when a hostile group was present. To support
his position, he investigated groups of friends in a nurses'
school, using a sociometric questionnaire and other sources
of information. The members of these groups were asked
to write down, while listening to a record, within a set time

limit, as many names of towns as possible. They then watched a rather blurred projection of each list, and were asked to judge the number of names of towns on each list. As predicted, there was a positive correlation between sociometric status and overestimation of attributed achievement. The groups then repeated the experimental task, some in the presence of a hostile group, the others in the presence of a friendly group. In this second session, both overestimation and its correlation with sociometric status increased only in the presence of a hostile group.

The mere reference to a rival group has effects upon the pattern of influence within a group. In order to study the effect of the evocation of a rival group upon the self-picture of a membership group, we asked students at a school of architecture, in a control condition, to give individually their opinions of the school, and then, after discussion, to give common opinions in groups of four, before finally again giving their individual opinions. In the experimental condition, the subjects were in each case asked also to estimate the opinion likely to be expressed by the pupils of another school of high standing, about the subjects' school (Doise, 1969a). The effects of referring to the other group were various. The picture of one's own group became more clearly defined in the experimental condition. Subjects adhered more frequently to their group norms, and the extremists, i.e. those subjects who had expressed their opinion more clearly, enjoyed higher sociometric status and had more influence than was the case when the other school was not referred to. The mere reference to another group therefore means that one's opinions concerning one's own group become more extreme while, at the same time, the members of the group give special status to the most extreme among them.

Deconchy (1971) asked students at a Catholic institution to answer a questionnaire in which they were invited to give free associations in response to the stimulus word 'God'. One half of the students were told that the questionnaire came from an anti-religious group, while the other half were told that it came from a religious body. In the latter case, the associations were richer and more varied. In the case of the anti-religious group questionnaire, the students restricted themselves largely to associations indicated in the catechism. In other words, faced with a hostile group, the members of a religious group take refuge in orthodoxy. It was also the case in this experiment, that reference to another group made the existing group structure more salient.

REPRESENTATION DURING GROUP INTERACTION

Groups solidify, divide and integrate, come together or draw apart in their perceptions, attitudes and behaviour. These phenomena cannot be understood simply in terms of the conflict, communality or hierarchy of interests. There may be discrimination between groups even when a conflict of interests is not inevitable. Some findings actually suggest that discrimination occurs of its own accord. It is implied that intergroup relations form the basis of norms and representations. Here we do indeed have examples of social psychological processes showing intrinsic development. They develop into institutions and ideologies which outlive the 'objective' situations to which they owe their origin. It is therefore necessary to complement Sherif's basic presupposition, according to which group aims determine the social psychological nature of the interactions between the groups. Our view is as follows. Goals determine the characteristics of group interaction by way of the representations to which they give rise. Social representations are of particular significance in group interaction. Their content may be modified by the nature of intergroup relations, but they themselves also influence the development of these relations, by anticipating their development and justifying their nature. Although representations are determined by interaction, they in turn also influence the course of interaction. We shall try to demonstrate this point in a study of the development of representations in intergroup relations.

Selective representation

Avigdor (1953), by manipulating the relations between youth clubs rehearsing for a theatrical performance, studied the influence of the nature of these relations on the content of intergroup representations. She arranged her situations so that some clubs interacted with one another either favourably or unfavourably. An example of negative or unfavourable interaction is provided by the case in which two groups had to rehearse their play at the same time and on the same stage. In this case, negative characteristics were attributed to members of the out-group. This attribution was, however, selective; the qualities, the nature of which might justifiably induce hostile behaviour (e.g. cheating, selfish), were those more frequently attributed to the members of the other group than to the members of one's own group. There was no such clear difference in the attribution of less relevant negative characteristics (e.g. slovenly, depressed).

Other studies, using before-and-after measures, also indicate that the representations which groups have of each other develop with the development of relations between the groups. Sherif provides an example of the relation between the nature of representations and changes in the relations between group projects. Wilson, Chun and Kayatani (1965) confirm that it is not just any aspects of representations which change. Their subjects, who interacted in the complexly motivated game already referred to, described, both before and after the experiment, the opposing pair, their partner and themselves, on four different scales. One of the scales was concerned with relatively co-operative, competitive, hostile or generous motives. The others had to do with social characteristics, general abilities and qualities of personality. The change in the picture of the other group was highly selective, and was relevant only to motivation. After interaction, the other group was perceived as more competitive and more hostile, while perception of one's partner changed in the opposite direction. Wilson and Kayatani (1968) explain these findings (verified by a second experiment), in terms of a projective mechanism which would prevent subjects from noticing undesirable motives in their own group, but allow them to project such motives on to the other group, although in fact both groups behaved identically. The other group is therefore held responsible for the development of the particular form of intergroup relations.

Justificatory representation

Both Avigdor (1953) and Wilson and Kayatani (1968) attribute to intergroup representation the function of justifying a given behaviour with respect to the other group.

The study of stereotypes confirms this interpretation. The similarities across countries in respect of stereotypes having to do with different groups in the same low economic position suggests that such stereotypes have everywhere the function of maintaining the economic, sexual and cultural distance which the dominant groups wish to preserve in relation to the dominated. When in the United States, white pupils underestimate the scholastic achievement of black pupils (Clarke and Campbell, 1955), and when white policemen overestimate the crime rate among the black population (Kephart, 1954), it seems very likely that such opinions serve the function of justifying a state of segregation. Such justificatory mechanisms of projection are certainly involved in the image current in Western countries, of the countries of the Third World (Preiswerk and Perret, 1975).

The representation which members form of their own group has a similar role. It serves to protect the uniqueness of the group. Thus, in South Africa, Hindus admit their 'inferiority' in relation to whites in scientific and economic fields, but claim superiority in spiritual, social and practical fields (Mann, 1963). A comparable form of selectivity can be seen in overvaluation of its own achievement by a group. Bass (1965) asked groups to carry out different tasks which varied in respect of their relevance to the existing predispositions of the members. The groups did not overestimate their performances on the different tasks to the same degree. They were especially prone to overestimate in the case of tasks which were relevant to their existing predispositions. This search for superiority in a particular area is even more subtly reflected in Lemaine's studies (1966). Two groups of children in holiday camps took part in competitive activities. There was a treasure hunt, the building of a hut and the planning of a holiday camp. One group was always at a disadvantage; it had fewer resources than the other and its overall performance was therefore likely to be inferior to that of the other group. Although such groups have a tendency to make themselves exclusive, they are nonetheless active in the search for, and, if need be, the discovery of dimensions in respect of which their performance may be judged superior to that of the other group.

Although distortions such as these are characteristic of the images which groups hold of one another, these images still retain a certain degree of objectivity. Defining 'objective' as what both membership group and other groups agree upon, Peabody (1968) distinguishes between objectivity in this sense, and the evaluative implications which mediate intergroup judgments. Let us consider an example. A person who tends to keep a close eye on his expenditure may be judged to be 'thrifty' or 'stingy'; one who spends freely may be judged to be 'generous' or 'extravagant'. The same characteristic is judged more positively by the members of the membership group than by the others. Peabody confirmed his finding for different ethnic groups in the Phillippines by using pairs of bipolar scales, with both objective and evaluative poles opposed for each scale, (e.g. thrifty–extravagant; generous–stingy). The algebraic sums of the responses to these scales were in general more positive for descriptions which members gave of their own group, than for descriptions of their group by other groups; this would seem to indicate an evaluative bias in favour of one's own group. But the value of the differences in the responses to such scales is most often systematically different from zero,

which indicates a tendency to objectivity. This would indicate that an aspect of 'social' reality defined in terms of
consensus finds expression in intergroup judgments, while
still leaving scope for evaluative bias.

Anticipatory representation

The way in which groups elaborate different kinds of representation depends on the relations between the groups. The
representations serve the function of justifying a particular
form of development, while enabling groups to retain their
particular nature and identity. If this is the case, the function
of representations cannot be limited to following, and
adapting to, relations between groups. On the contrary, the
representation plays a part in determining this very development of intergroup relations, by actively anticipating it.

In two studies, we found, before group interaction, that
characteristics justifying a competitive attitude were already
attributed to the out-group. This was the case in the Grenoble experiment on the differently constituted pairs (Doise,
1969d), which interacted in the mixed motivation game
previously described. After an introduction to the experimental situation, the subjects were asked to describe the
other group, their partner and themselves, on a French or
German version of the motivation scale used by Wilson,
Chun and Kayatani (1965). As Figure 7 indicates, even
before interaction, in each case, subjects attributed fewer
co-operative motives to the other group than to their partners
or to themselves. Mere anticipation of future interaction was
sufficient to create an image of the other groups which, in
turn, was bound to affect the behaviour of the subjects
toward these other groups. Because, in this kind of situation,
all the actors tend to develop the same kind of representation,
there is a cumulative effect, and the form of reality which
emerges as the end product corresponds to the representations which have served to elicit it. This reflects the
reification or self-fulfilment effect of social representations.
Figure 7 also shows that the same objective behaviour leads

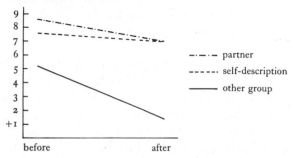

Figure 7. Mean level of co-operation attributed to oneself, one's partner and the other group before and after playing a mixed-motive game. The scale measures the mean value of the sums of eight bipolar scales from −3 to +3, concerned with co-operative motivation. The findings from the three experimental conditions have been combined. (From Doise, 1969d)

to a devaluation in the representation of one's antagonists but not in the representation of the members of one's own group.

The second study (Doise and Weinberger, 1972–3) concerned with the anticipatory aspect of intergroup representations will be described in detail in the final chapter. It was found that two boys who were opposed in a competitive situation to two girls, projected a more unfavourable and more feminine image of the girls than when boys and girls had to act together. When some action is to be undertaken, representations justifying this action are brought to bear. They therefore represent a link between past and future.

The aim of groups in competitive interaction is to produce a better result, often qualitatively different from that of the competing group, as indeed Lemaine (1974) has confirmed. The subjects' representations foreshadow the outcome. The product of one's own group is not only overestimated, but as Blake and Mouton (1962a) further show, the members of a group are inclined to minimise the similarities between the product of their own group and the product of the other group. The group construes images of the position which it would like to attain, and these images filter the group's representation of the existing situation. Thus the wished-for situation is created in imagination. Any judge going against this representation would simply be regarded as prejudiced and rejected as such.

Selectivity, justification and anticipation are clearly not independent aspects of intergroup representations. They involve the same kind of dynamic process. Representations, by providing a certain image of the other group, attributing certain kinds of motive to it, pave the way for action with respect to that group. Just as the ideomotor images described by psychophysiology include the first step toward their realisation, an intergroup representation also functions as an initial form of action in the social world. This function probably holds the key to the explanation of the sharpness of the dominant traits of intergroup relations. These traits transform the representations into a powerful tool with which the group defines its uniqueness and marks out its contribution to history. The intensification of stereotypes, which can often be observed at a period of crisis, may represent the beginning of the process by which a group again finds its place in, and takes part in the social environment.

The studies reported in this chapter can scarcely be said to have cast much light upon social psychological processes. They have simply shown how it is possible to create experimentally social psychological situations in the field of intergroup relations. The situations described did indeed activate norms and representations already operative in a social setting while at the same time activating individual acts and judgments. But at the theoretical level, it must be said that the integration of sociology and psychology is relatively speaking, overlooked. This does not mean that the experiments did not make a real contribution to scientific thinking. Sherif's theoretical formulations allow us a better understanding of the vicissitudes of war and alliances between peoples. Some of the experiments provide some explanation of the conditions in which ideological representations, of the kind which we have called justificatory, emerge. They thus illustrate the sound basis on which certain conceptions of the nature of ideology have been founded.

Such studies, however, do not find much favour with sociologists, who remain unimpressed by the aspects of their subject matter which psychologists, working in a given society, have tried to reproduce experimentally. Frequently, indeed, social psychologists seem to make no real effort to place their findings in the wider context of the dynamics of a given society. It can, however, be argued that the studies which we have cited may, in respect of their illustrative function, promote more penetrating reflection on the function of the sociologist. From one point of view at least, their subject matter is more tangible than that of the sociologist.

Investigators who work at the purely psychological level are not impressed, either, by the findings of the studies reported. They are used to demonstrating in a more detailed way, the operation of cognitive, perceptual or affective processes. To date, social psychologists have not attained such a level of explanation. One may, indeed, wonder whether this can ever be achieved. Are the 'laws' they discover not inevitably of a more statistical nature? Although we are not necessarily convinced that this is the case, we nevertheless recognise that the task of social psychology does not consist primarily in clear conceptualisation of the individual repercussions involved in any form of social interaction.

Misunderstandings between psychologists and sociologists are not inevitable. To resolve such misunderstandings, social psychologists must extend their studies and concentrate on social psychological processes, which are neither exclusively psychological nor exclusively sociological, but apposite at both levels of explanation. With regard to the studies we have described, we shall therefore have to indicate in detail what they have to contribute to the integration of psychology and sociology. We shall attempt to do so in the next chapter in which we shall describe the social psychological process of category differentiation.

2

Category differentiation

Social psychology has been able experimentally to cast light upon the kind of processes which form a bridge between psychology and sociology. The last two chapters of this book will be devoted to showing that this is so in the special field of intergroup relations. First, however, we shall describe the process of category differentiation. This is a process which has developed in the natural history of species, and which helps the human being to structure his social environment. It also involves a social psychological process which takes account of the way in which social reality is structured. This chapter will therefore present a social psychological definition of category differentiation. The next chapter will report some recent experimental studies concerned with the processes involved, at the level of behaviour, representations and evaluations between groups, under differing conditions.

A PSYCHOLOGICAL PROCESS

Studies in the field of perception produced the psychological definition of the process of category differentiation. These studies were concerned with the way in which an individual, in a given field, construed his experience of his environment. This experience, while psychological in origin, equally has its place in phylogenetic and social history. Holzkamp (1973) has again drawn attention to this complex situation, which involves the historical setting of such experience and the individual development of perception. The following observations on the phylogenesis and sociogenesis of perception are based on Holzkamp's suggestions.

The natural history of the process

The differentiation within the organism of its experience of its environment develops in the course of phylogenesis as an important mechanism in the struggle for the survival of species. In the process of interaction with the environment which characterises the metabolic processes of living creatures, there is a critical point at which an organism no longer reacts only to the things which are immediately necessary for the maintenance of life, but becomes equally responsive to stimuli which are not concerned directly in the chemical and biological changes involved in metabolism (Leontiev, 1973). Such responsiveness, for example that of the spider reacting to vibrations of its web (ibid, p. 155) allows a more effective orientation toward the factors necessary for survival, on the basis of stimuli such as sounds, smells and light intensity which are objectively associated with the immediately indispensable factors. There is therefore a qualitative difference between a protozoan organism which responds only to the metabolites in the fluid which constitutes its world, and a more highly developed organism to which various signs, not directly related to its metabolism, are still relevant to an orientation toward the organism's sources of survival. These differentiations at the perceptual level, in so far as they are based on genuine relations between factors in the environment, therefore represent an effective weapon in the struggle for the survival of species. They also presuppose the development of specific receptors.

To outline a phylogenetic history of perception would scarcely be relevant. We should like simply to make the point that, from the very beginning, perception implies the existence of relations between phenomena of a very different nature. This is an important aspect of our definition of the process of category differentiation. When, in the course of evolution, the activities or predispositions of creatures of the

same species become important for the survival of the individual members of the species, this characteristic of
perception retains its significance. The development of
processes of communication requires a new development of
sensory and communicatory organs permitting the apprehension and communication of new differentiations related
to states of the organism.

With the appearance of man, natural history becomes
more specifically social history; the development of communal tools is evidence of this. This new development in
behaviour is accompanied by further development of perception. Perception creates objects independent of current
action, and these objects are recognised as such. Perception
thus becomes objective and also social in nature. It becomes
in effect equivalent to the apprehension of the meanings
which become attached to man-made objects in the organised action of any collectivity. At the same time, it distinguishes the activities of different participants in collective
tasks, such as that of tracking and trapping game, to cite an
example borrowed by Holzkamp (1973) from Leontiev (1973).
Thus, social perception evolves with the development of the
organisation of labour. Moreover, the particular position
occupied by individuals in this organisation facilitates the
development of specific forms of sensory activity and particular ideological representations. In the ontogenetic development of man, his biological inheritance thus combines
with the assimilation of meanings which have crystallised
throughout social history and which are both mediated by
language and incorporated in man-made objects.

Although we agree with Holzkamp's insistence on the
necessity of viewing the study of perception within the
framework of the particular social structure involved, we also
feel, with Holzkamp himself, that there are perceptual
processes which are characteristic of the whole human race
and which can be studied as such. A knowledge of these
common processes is an indispensable condition for the
elucidation of the specific characteristic of the psychological
phenomena which appear in any particular society.

Only when we have succeeded in isolating them from the events of natural history in determining the main factors underlying the particular qualities of the socially determined subjective aspects of human life . . . may we proceed to a third stage in which we can, by factual analysis . . . define cases which are not only specific to humans as social beings, but which are specific to human social life in a bourgeois society (Holzkamp, 1973, p. 54).

This general analysis is, however, inevitably abstract and is inadequate to deal with man as a concrete phenomenon, moulded by his membership of a given social group (Holzkamp and Schurig, 1973, p. xlvii).

The psychological process of category differentiation is one of these general processes of abstraction which enable one to account for the way in which real living men come to perceive reality as they do, and how they manage to adopt a relatively stable position in the face of the ambiguities and uncertainties of any given situation. Like the regularities described by Piaget (1969), the organisational factors indicated by Holzkamp (1973, pp. 312ff) enable the organism to overcome the limitations inherent in the specific perception of aspects of reality. These organisational effects are closer to the level of phylogenetic inheritance than the assimilation of the specific characteristics of a particular social system. 'In individual development, organisational effects are mainly the result of the ontogenetic development of phylogenetic data; the process of assimilation plays only a secondary role' (Holzkamp, 1973, p. 317).

An important mechanism in perceptual organisation is the accentuation of differences.

Closed contours, in the absence of other information, are not perceived as lines, but as boundaries which separate an object from its background . . . The difference in brightness between the contiguous surfaces is accentuated in perception . . . The same is true for differences in size . . . Small figures in the visual field, like dots relatively close to one another, are perceived as units. Meaningfulness also tends to produce groupings which are closely organised internally and clearly delimited from the surrounding field.

The result, as far as perceptual organisation is concerned, is that – under imperfect perceptual conditions – there is an under-estimation of the extent to which the figure is differentiated. The threshold for the recognition of actual differences in colour and luminosity rises when such differences occur within a figure, and is much lower in a background setting...Conversely, wholes consisting of small figures are regarded as single figures when the parts are identical or similar...It is almost as if perception looked to the likeness of small figures as an index of their belongingness to one particular entity' (ibid, pp. 314ff).

This passage is accompanied by a number of references to experiments on perception. These experiments were carried out by investigators in the Gestalt tradition, making theoretical assumptions which Holzkamp does not share. But the notion of internal homogeneity and differentiation from what lies without, has been adopted by a different line of research on perception which, following Bruner, uses the concept of categorisation. 'Perception involves an act of categorization...we stimulate an organism with some appropriate input and he responds by referring the input to some class of things or events' (Bruner, 1957, p. 123). Bruner's studies, on both perception and cognition, have particularly emphasised the way in which similarities and differences are used as a basis for inferring category characteristics. Bruner also emphasises the similarity between perception and cognition.

The experiment by Bruner most frequently referred to by social psychologists, however, is not directly concerned with the process of categorisation. Since it formed the basis of Tajfel's conceptualisation of this process, which we shall presently examine, we shall summarise briefly the well-known experiment by Bruner and Goodman (1947). It was designed to test two predictions based on the hypothesis of a relation between the value of an object and the overestimation of its size. It was predicted that coins would appear bigger than valueless tokens of the same diameter, and that this phenomenon of accentuation would be more marked among poor children than among well-off children. In the light of several replications of the experiment, we cannot conclude that the latter prediction has been verified beyond dispute. In any case, we are more directly interested in the results which confirm the former prediction. The experimenters did indeed find that the size of the coins was overestimated in relation to the size of neutral tokens. Several other studies confirm this finding, but not always significantly in respect of the smallest coins presented to the subject. It was in an attempt to give a more systematic account of the findings of these various studies that Tajfel developed his model of the categorisation process.

Tajfel's formulation

Bruner's work was referred to as the 'New Look' in perception. His studies introduced a social factor into a field which had hitherto been regarded as purely psychological, or psychophysiological. A new conception emerged of certain perceptual mechanisms which had already been investigated by Gestalt psychologists. Tajfel (1959) clearly and decisively defined, in six hypotheses, one of the individual mechanisms by which the social characteristics of certain stimuli influence the perception of the physical characteristics of these stimuli. Tajfel's propositions were expressed in the form of the following experimental predictions.

(1) When a variation in value is correlated in a series of stimuli with a variation in a physical dimension, the judged differences in this physical dimension between the elements of the series will be larger than in a series which is identical with regard to the physical magnitudes of the stimuli, and in which the stimuli do not possess the attribute of value.

(2) When differences in value exist in a series of stimuli, but are in no way correlated with the variation in a physical dimension, these differences in value will have no effect on the judged relationships between the physical magnitudes of the stimuli of the series.

(3) When a classification in terms of an attribute other than the physical dimension which is being judged is superimposed on a series of stimuli in such a way that one part of the physical series tends to fall consistently into one class, and the other into the other class, judgments of physical magnitudes of the stimuli falling into

the distinct classes will show a shift in the directions determined by the class membership of the stimuli, when compared with judgments of a series identical with respect to this physical dimension, on which such a classification is not superimposed.

(4) When a classification in terms of an attribute other than the physical dimension which is being judged is superimposed on a series of stimuli, and the changes in the physical magnitudes of the stimuli bear no consistent relationship to the assignment of the stimuli to the distinct classes, this classification will have no effect on the judged relationships in the physical dimension between the stimuli of the series.

(5) When a classification in terms of an attribute other than the physical dimension which is being judged is superimposed on a series of stimuli in such a way that one part of the physical series tends to fall consistently into one class, and the other into the other class, and this classification is of inherent value or of emotional relevance to the subject, judgments of physical magnitudes of the stimuli falling into the distinct classes will show a shift in directions determined by the class membership of the stimuli when compared with judgments of a series identical with respect to this physical dimension, on which such a classification is not superimposed; this shift will be more pronounced than the shift referred to in (3) above.

(6) When a classification in terms of an attribute other than the physical dimension which is being judged is superimposed on a series of stimuli, this classification being of inherent value or of emotional relevance to the subject, and the changes in the physical dimension bear no consistent relationship to the assignment of the stimuli to the distinct classes, this classification will have no effect on the judged relationships in the physical dimensions between the stimuli falling into the distinct classes (Tajfel, 1959, pp. 20ff).

Since, in our view, these propositions concern a process which reflects the psychological aspect of a social psychological process, it is important to see how far they are supported by empirical findings.

Experimental confirmation

The experiment by Bruner and Goodman (1947) to which we have already referred, provides confirmation of the first prediction. The diameter of the American one cent, five cent, ten cent, twenty-five cent and fifty cent coins varies directly with their value. On the basis of the findings of Bruner and Goodman, and those of other investigators, Tajfel (1959) is justified in claiming that differences in the size of coins are exaggerated compared with differences in the size of neutral tokens. The second prediction has not really been subjected to systematic investigation. Some results, however, such as those of Lysak and Gilchrist (1955), which find no consistent difference between judgments of the size of dollar bills and judgments of the size of similar valueless sheets of paper, are consistent with the prediction. All dollar bills are the same size, and there is therefore no relation between their value and their size; accordingly, there is no reason to expect any overestimation of their size.

Tajfel's other four hypotheses have more solid experimental backing. Experiments have been carried out specifically to verify them. These experiments, the most significant of which have been carried out by Tajfel himself and his colleagues, are directly relevant to the psychological process of category differentiation. We shall describe in detail an experiment by Tajfel and Wilkes (1963) which supports predictions (3) and (4), and a replication of this experiment by Marchand (1970) which also confirms Tajfel's last two predictions.

With reference to the third and fourth predictions of the 1959 formulation, Tajfel and Wilkes (1963) introduce a new prediction – when a classification superimposed on a series of stimuli is correlated with their positions on a physical dimension, not only will the differences between stimuli belonging to the different classes be emphasised (hypothesis 4), but the similarities between stimuli belonging to the same category will also be exaggerated. The two main predictions to be tested concerning the effect of a dichotomous classification were therefore as follows. (1) There will be an accentuation of inter-category differences and of intra-category similarities when a classification is superimposed on stimuli the positions of which on a physical dimension are correlated with their category memberships. (2) These accentuations will not occur when there is no systematic relation between category membership and the physical qualities being judged.

Two secondary hypotheses were also tested: (a) the effects of similarities and differences should be greater when category membership is more salient; (b) there should be a similar increase in the effect when subjects are familiar in advance with the classes of stimuli to be judged. We should, perhaps, before going on to describe the experimental procedure, observe that the categorisation effects involving emphasis on similarities 'within' and differences 'between' are comparable to those described by Holzkamp in the quotation in which he emphasises the effects of differentiation. Holzkamp, however, would probably not subscribe to the second supplementary hypothesis of Tajfel and Wilkes. According to Holzkamp, discrimination is one of the organising factors which compensate for the deficiencies of perception in an unfamiliar situation (Holzkamp, 1973, pp. 306–14).

The experimental stimuli used by Tajfel and Wilkes consisted of a series of eight lines each differing from the next by about five per cent of its length. The shortest line was 162 mm long and the longest line 229 mm long. Every line was drawn diagonally on a white rectangular card. According to the experimental conditions, the lines were systematically classified (condition 1), classified at random (condition 2), or not classified at all (condition 3).

In condition (1), for each of the shortest four lines, the letter A appeared in the middle of the card; for the longest four lines, there was a letter B. There was therefore a perfect point-biserial correlation between the length of the lines and their membership of category A or category B. The predicted accentuations of differences and similarities should therefore be found in this case.

In condition (2), the classification was not correlated with the length of the lines. The lines were presented along with the letters A or B, but in such a way that for half of the presentations of each line, one of these letters appeared on the card, while the other letter appeared on the card for the other half of the presentations. The letter A or B appeared with each line by chance. In this condition, there was no systematic relation between category membership and length. The categorisation process could not, therefore, affect the subjects' judgments.

In condition (3), no letter was associated with the lines. The absence of categorisation should therefore have meant that there was no accentuation of similarities and differences.

Common to the three experimental conditions was the fact that the eight stimulus lines were presented to the subject several times, in random order. At each presentation, the subjects estimated the length of the line.

The experimental conditions were put into effect in different ways, involving more or fewer predetermined presentations of the lines to be judged, and in two experimental sessions, in order to test the supplementary hypotheses. We shall consider here the experimental procedure which yielded the clearest results. This involved three series of presentations of stimuli and of judgments. We reproduce the findings of the last series of judgments in Table 8, which gives the averages of the judgments made in respect of the shortest four and longest four stimuli. The differences between the two categories are greater in condition 1 than they are in actual fact, and greater than they appear in conditions 2 and 3. Again, Figure 8 indicates how the inter-category difference appears in the case of borderline stimuli between the two classes. When categorisation is relevant (condition 1), the difference between the responses of subjects is approximately 150 per cent above the actual difference, while when categorisation is irrelevant, the difference emerging from the judgments made is slightly less than the actual difference.

Hypotheses three and four, as formulated in the 1959 model, are thus confirmed by this experiment. Differences are indeed accentuated when there is a correlation between

Table 8. *Mean actual and estimated lengths (in cm) of the four shortest and four longest stimuli in different experimental conditions used by Tajfel and Wilkes*

Mean lengths	Short stimuli	Long stimuli	Difference
Actual	17.475	21.225	3.750
Estimated in condition 1	18.175	22.600	4.425
Estimated in conditions 2 and 3	18.350	21.900	3.550

SOURCE: after Tajfel and Wilkes, 1963, Table 4.

category membership and the physical characteristic to be judged. They are not accentuated when there is no such correlation. The accentuation of intra-class similarities, however, is not significantly different in the two experimental conditions. The first supplementary hypothesis was not confirmed either, but the second did receive experimental support; when an experimental session was immediately followed by another session, inter-class differentiation was intensified.

The question is whether we can conclude that the accentuation of similarities within classes does not occur. If Tajfel's experiment failed to reveal such accentuation, this might have been because of the nature of the experimental task. We cannot exclude the possibility that the subjects in the different experimental conditions introduced supplementary classifications of certain stimuli, not necessarily in a mutually consistent way. It is thus possible that they distinguished the shortest and longest lines with respect to the others. Such 'spontaneous' classifications might explain, for instance, the slight overestimation of the difference between stimuli (7) and (8), which was also found in another experiment which will be described (Marchand, 1970), and which in the present case is represented in Figure 8. It

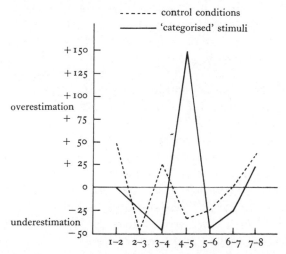

Figure 8. Overestimation and underestimation of differences between adjacent stimuli (in percentages). (After Tajfel and Wilkes, 1963, p. 111)

therefore seems important, before examining the experimental status of hypotheses five and six, to look for further confirmation of the accentuation of intra-class similarities.

The overestimation of similarities within categories superimposed upon a physical dimension has in fact been confirmed by other experiments. We shall describe one such experiment which used very different stimulus material, and was carried out at Haskins' phonetics research laboratory. It has been reported by Brown (1965, pp. 260–5). Haskins' laboratory is concerned with studying the acoustic characteristics of different English phonemes, with the aid of an acoustic spectrograph transforming emitted sounds into visual traces. The spectrograms thus obtained can in turn be translated into sounds. To clarify the specific nature of certain phonemes, spectrograms were simplified and systematically modified. On this basis, it was possible to deduce what characteristics were necessary for a reproduced sound to be recognised as a phoneme. Although the characteristics of English consonants are in general very complex and varied, some groups of phonemes fortunately vary in one dimension only. This is the case for the consonants b, d and g, which are characterised by certain systematic variations in the acoustic frequencies of the vowels which follow them. Thus it has been possible to construct spectrograms which differ among themselves by intervals of 120 cps on an acoustic dimension. For English sounds, this continuum covers a range from b to d to g, and each zone includes at least four or five intervals of 120 cps.

The categorisation system was relevant when these phonemes were presented. On the one hand, the stimuli were placed on a continuum at regular intervals, while on the other hand the same stimuli were also grouped systematically into adjoining categories. The question is whether there is accentuation of intra-category similarities and of inter-category differences when auditory perception is involved. An experiment described by Brown (1965) indicates that this is indeed so. By confronting subjects with triads of auditory stimuli, A–B–X, where X is equal to A or B, and asking subjects to say whether X is equal to A or B, an index of discrimination can be obtained by counting the number of correct identifications of X. We can thus confirm whether discrimination is equally efficient for all the pairs of auditory stimuli separated by the same interval in terms of cps. This is in fact not the case. For example, in the case of two stimuli separated by 240 cps which belong to different phonetic classes (e.g., b and d, or d and g), the judged differences are significantly more frequently correct than in the case of judged differences between two stimuli, separated by the same 240 cps interval but belonging to the same class b, d or g. We therefore find here accentuation of both inter-class differences and intra-class similarities. Studies of colour vision in different cultures which may classify the colour spectrum in different ways, also indicate that there is a relation between codification and colour discrimination as suggested by the categorisation model (see Tajfel, 1969, pp. 373ff).

It is difficult to imagine a situation, even an experimental situation, which does not carry value implications in respect of the different elements involved, and therefore in respect of the stimuli which the subjects are asked to judge, but it is also true that the experiments so far reported were not intended to study the effect of value on the process of categorisation in the strict sense. Tajfel's fifth and sixth predictions (1959) did concern this issue, but it was only much later that an experiment was devised to test these predictions. Marchand (1970) carried out an experiment very similar to that already described by Tajfel and Wilkes (1963), also intended to verify the findings of Tajfel and Wilkes with somewhat different material. The variables studied were – (a) random classification of a series of stimuli on a physical dimension; (b) systematic classification of these stimuli with respect to position on a physical dimension but without reference to their position on a superimposed value dimension; (c) systematic classification with respect to both physical and value dimensions.

The stimuli used by Marchand were squares of which the sides varied gradually from 5 to 17.9 cm. The stimuli were classified not only by having the letter A or B attributed to them, but also by having the squares coloured blue or green. Moreover, these two classifications were experimentally counterbalanced, so that the experimental design included four conditions. (1) Control condition without any systematic classification. (2) Condition with systematic classification with respect to area but not with respect to value. (3) Condition similar to condition 2, but including a value dimension uncorrelated with the physical classification. (4) Condition in which a value dimension was added, correlated with the area of the squares and with the basic classification. The aspect of this experiment which most concerns us is the effect of the value dimension. This was manipulated in conditions 3 and 4 of the experiment. The experimental stimuli were presented as targets in a darts game. For the subjects in condition 4, in which classification, area and value were assigned to the targets, the smallest four squares were assigned negative values, decreasing with the size of the square, while the largest four squares were assigned positive

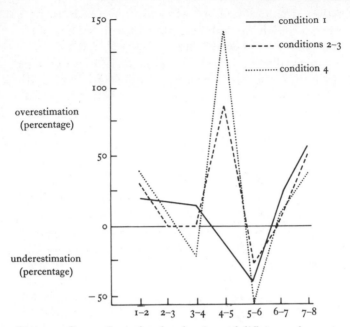

Figure 9. Comparison of real and estimated differences between adjacent stimuli for the four conditions of Marchand's experiment (1970, p. 270)

values corresponding to their position in the series. The same values appeared on the target-squares in condition 3, but were assigned at random. In the first two conditions, no darts game was involved, and value was not manipulated.

The findings in the first two conditions confirm those of Tajfel and Wilkes (1963). There was no significant difference between condition 2 and condition 3, which indicates that the non-systematic addition of value has no effect. On the other hand, the addition of value correlated with category membership increases the accentuation of differences between stimuli belonging to the two different classes. Figure 9 illustrates these findings by giving the differences observed in subjects' judgments and comparing these differences with the actual differences, in terms of percentage.

Marchand's experiment really sews up the problem concerned. It is well-known that the theoretical formulation of the categorisation process put forward by Tajfel (1959) was based upon studies of judgments of the size of coins. Marchand shows that the model holds in the case where there is an experimentally contrived relation between area, classification and value. The description of the psychological process of categorisation, as given by Tajfel (1959) in his last four hypotheses, has thus solid experimental support. There are also other experimental findings which support the viability of this model. And it can be shown that results which at first sight do not seem to support it have in fact been obtained under conditions which do not allow the process to function properly. Reference may be made to authors such as Eiser and Stroebe (1972).

THE PSYCHOLOGICAL ORGANISATION OF THE SOCIAL ENVIRONMENT

When an experimenter organises his experimental stimuli in a particular way, or when a culture divides up the spectrum of colour or of sound in a particular way, the results do of course represent a facet of social reality. It may therefore appear arbitrary to introduce a section specifically devoted to the study of the psychological aspects of the organisation of the social environment. This can, however, be justified. So far, the model proposed and the experiments reported have been concerned with purely physical stimuli such as lines, sounds, contours and areas. We must now enquire whether a different process may not be involved when we are concerned with judgments involving more immediately social material, such as opinions, persons, social groups and attitudes. We shall therefore describe some studies which indicate that the categorisation process is relevant to judgments of persons, and equally useful for the understanding of judgments of opinions or attitudes. The last group of studies are especially important because they suggest that the operation of the categorisation process is marked by a kind of asymmetry when it concerns judgments of objects which have social value.

The description of persons

There is a structural analogy between judgments of physical stimuli such as those used by Tajfel and Wilkes (1963) and the stereotyped judgments of persons based upon their membership of ethnic or national groups. In this field, stereotyping represents the attributing of similar characteristics to different members of the same group, without sufficient account being taken of possible differences among the members of the group.

Let us consider in more detail the nature of judgments such as 'Nordics are tall' or 'Mediterranean people are small'. We are not concerned for the moment with any possible objective basis for such judgments; it is obvious that some Nordics are small and some Mediterranean people are tall. What we are interested in is the structure of the judgments of someone who expresses such a stereotype. For him, there is a connection, at least probabilistic and subjective, between belonging to the category 'Nordic' or 'Mediterranean' and position on a physical dimension, i.e. height. There is therefore a structural analogy between such judgments and those studied by Tajfel and Wilkes. The association with membership of social categories may similarly have implications for the positions of the members of these groups on a psychological dimension. For example, Orientals are regarded by many as more spiritualistic, Westerners as more materialistic. Such stereotypes also suppose the acceptance by those who use them, of a relation between membership of a category and the possession of a certain characteristic. The question is whether experiment confirms that stereotypes take shape in accordance with the laws of the categorisation process. This has to be shown empirically.

One fact which has been well established experimentally is that information about the category membership of a person has a strong influence on judgments made concerning that person, as is shown by Razran (1950). In the first part of his experiment, Razran presented 30 photographs of faces which were either pleasant or neutral with regard to ethnic characteristics. Subjects had to judge these faces on a five-point scale in respect of the criteria 'General liking, Beauty, Intelligence, Character, Ambition and Entertainingness'. In the second part of the experiment, two months later, the subjects were again shown the same photographs, but each photograph had attached a surname and first name. 5 of these names were Jewish, 5 Italian, 5 Irish and 15 'genuine' American. New photographs with names taken at random from a telephone directory were added to the names from the first part of the experiment. To show the effect of the information provided in the second part, we may simply refer to the changes in respect of the faces which were labelled 'Jewish'. The judgments which they received were 1.21 points less for sympathy, 0.81 less for character. On the other hand, their scores were 1.01 greater for ambition and 0.36 greater for intelligence. It is clear, therefore, that information concerning category membership does affect judgment.

Studies specifying the processes involved in these category judgments are less common, but we shall report two studies showing more or less directly how the categorisation process works in the description of persons of different nationality. One such study was carried out by Bruner and Perlmutter (1957) before Tajfel's statement of the process (1959). It was concerned with the formation of impressions of strangers. The following two hypotheses were tested. (1) The first impression made by a stimulus person A on another person B will be less influenced by A's category membership, the more varied have been B's previous contacts with different members of this category. (2) The category memberships which distinguish between a number of persons presented at the same time, will be more influential in the impression formed of each person, than when these persons are presented separately. The second hypothesis is clearly more relevant to the categorisation process as described by Tajfel than the first hypothesis, since Tajfel's formulation presupposes the simultaneous presence of several category memberships. We shall, however, also give the results relevant to the first hypothesis. They are relevant to a problem with which we shall ultimately be concerned, that of the differences between individual contacts and group contacts.

Bruner and Perlmutter tested their hypotheses with subjects in three different countries (United States, France and West Germany). Their experimental design included 36 experimental groups. Their experimental procedure was simple. Subjects had to describe fictitious persons who were presented to them as follows. 'He is a very typical. . . There is general agreement among those who know him that he is intelligent, energetic, and well-adjusted. Now 42 years old, he is married and lives in a large city in. . .' (Bruner and Perlmutter, 1957, p. 255). The first set of dots was filled in by a noun indicating an occupation and an adjective indicating the nationality of the person, e.g. French business man, or just by an indication of nationality, e.g. French. The latter set of dots was filled in by the name of one of the three countries. The experimental conditions consisted mainly of confronting the subjects with a stimulus person from their own country or from a foreign country, in order to test the first hypothesis, or with three stimulus persons of three different nationalities with the same occupation, to test the second hypothesis by comparing these multiple presentations with individual presentations. The presentation of the single person or of each of the three persons was followed by the issue of a sheet containing a list of 38 adjectives which were all more or less in keeping with the characteristics of being intelligent, energetic and well adjusted. The subjects were first asked to indicate which adjectives applied to the person described. Next, they were asked to say whether they had assigned these adjectives on the basis of the psychological traits mentioned in the presentation, or on the basis of the nationality or occupation of the stimulus person. They were allowed to give several reasons for each decision. Table 9 shows the mean number of traits assigned in each of the experimental conditions on the basis of the nationality of the person described.

Table 9. *Number of characteristics attributed as a function of the nationality of the person described*

Groups	French subjects		German subjects		American subjects	
	Foreign-ers	Com-patriots	Foreign-ers	Com-patriots	Foreign-ers	Com-patriots
1 person only	4.6	2.8	3.9	1.4	3.3	1.3
3 persons	6.8	6.8	6.6	4.5	5.2	4.3

SOURCE: Bruner and Perlmutter, 1957.

When subjects had to describe one person, he was in fact, as the first column of the table shows, most frequently described according to his nationality if he was a foreigner. These results were repeated in three countries, and confirm the first hypothesis. The second hypothesis is also confirmed, as indicated by the fact that the mean values in the lower line of Table 9 are higher than those in the upper line. Confrontation with persons of different nationality therefore seems to increase the salience of nationality. The results for French subjects indeed suggest that this fresh salience may be sufficient to offset the familiarisation effect implied by the first hypothesis.

Compared with the Razran type of experiment (1950), that of Bruner and Perlmutter is more informative about the categorisation process. It suggests conditions which may facilitate or inhibit the potential influence of information concerning category membership. When differences between categories are induced, images change. The operation of the process of categorisation becomes possible because of the salience which category memberships come to acquire. It is therefore not surprising if a foreigner is perceived in terms of his nationality, even when he is alone, since people may think that in this case, differentiation in terms of nationality is relevant. On the other hand, when a compatriot is present, there is no question of several nationalities being involved. Bruner and Perlmutter's first hypothesis is therefore not essential for explaining the overall difference between meeting a compatriot and meeting a foreigner. Meeting a stranger is in some ways comparable to the situation in which three persons of different nationality are presented.

We shall now describe an experiment which Tajfel himself considers relevant to the functioning of the categorisation process, concerned with the description of persons belonging to different national groups. The first part of this experiment (Tajfel, Sheikh and Gardner, 1964) had already been carried out independently by Sheikh before additional studies were carried out to verify the relevance of the categorisation process. Sheikh asked Canadian students to listen to four interviews. After each interview, the subjects described the person interviewed in terms of 25 seven-point scales. Four persons were interviewed and described; a Canadian and a Hindu who spoke about their favourite films, and another Canadian and another Hindu who were questioned about their favourite books. In the second part of the experiment, other subjects had to select, from the adjectives used in the scales for the first part of the experiment, which adjectives were particularly applicable to Hindus and which particularly applicable to Canadians. On the basis of the responses of this second group of subjects, it was determined what traits were associated with the two national group memberships, e.g. spiritualistic and religious with the Hindus and conservative and sociable with the Canadians. It was also possible to indicate those traits for which there was no relation to membership of the Hindu group, such as sociable or sycophantic, or to membership of the Canadian group, such as subtle and spiritualistic. These data provided Tajfel with an illustration of the importance of the categorisation process.

The authors thus had the following information. They knew the category memberships of the stimulus persons and they knew which traits, of the 25 traits used to describe these persons, were generally related to each group membership.

This was enough at least to confirm the aspect of the categorisation process concerned with the accentuation of intra-category similarities. This accentuation is to be expected for traits which are correlated with category membership, and should not occur in the case of traits which are not thus correlated. Such a difference between relevant traits and non-relevant traits was indeed found. When we compare the mean differences between the scores which the Hindus obtained for traits typical of their group and the mean differences for non-typical traits, we find the former differences significantly less. The same thing holds in the case of the Canadians. In each case, there were smaller differences, or, to put it the other way round, greater similarities, in respect of characteristics related to the stereotype than in respect of characteristics not so related. Tajfel's formulation, therefore, in so far as it refers to intra-category similarities, covers the findings of the experiment which we have just described. But how? Is it because the intrinsic dynamics of the categorisation process are reflected in the subjects' judgments, biasing them in the expected direction, or is it because the stereotypes applied by the subjects in the second part of the experiment are objectively accurate and the stimulus persons in the first part simply embody these stereotypes? The experiment of Tajfel, Sheikh and Gardner provides no answer to this question. We cannot reject the hypothesis that the two representatives of each group actually were more alike in respect of the stereotyped traits than in respect of the non-stereotyped traits. On the basis of this experiment alone, all that can be concluded, in formal or structural terms, is that the categorisation model is applicable. Other experiments are required to show that the dynamic process of accentuation of intra-category similarities has its own intrinsic basis, which is relevant to the creation of objective reality as well as to the development of judgments. In the following chapter, we shall report some such experiments.

The assessment of opinions and attitudes

We have no intention of discussing the different models which have been put forward to explain certain character-istics of 'social judgments'. There are many such models. Eiser and Stroebe (1972) have described and discussed those which are essentially adaptations of models developed for physical judgments. Our aim is less ambitious. We want, first of all, to illustrate the operation of the categorisation process in a different field. The first study which we shall report attempts to show that the categorisation process, when it is involved in judgments concerning opinions and attitudes, which are always value-loaded, is affected by the values held by those who make the judgments. We shall then report two further studies which show how such factors work. The three studies which we shall report were all carried out by Eiser, a former associate of Tajfel, and are described in the book already referred to by Eiser and Stroebe on categorisation and social judgment.

Thurstone and Chave's technique for the measurement of attitudes (1929) has long been used by social psychologists. It consists, first of all, of submitting to judges a number of statements relevant to the issue being studied. The judges are asked to classify the statements according to their favour-ability or unfavourability with regard to the object of the attitude being studied. The judges rate the statements in terms of a given number of classes so that the statements are evenly divided between those more or less favourable and unfavourable to the object of the attitude, and that there is approximately the same distance between categories with respect to favourability. On the basis of the ratings of a number of judges, a small number of statements can be selected representative of different degrees of the attitude concerned. This new series of statements forms a scale. According as the subjects whose attitude we want to assess agree with certain of these statements which the judges have rated as more or less favourable to the object of the attitude, we conclude that the attitude of the subjects themselves is more or less favourable.

Thurstone and Chave (1929) assumed that the judges classified the statements systematically and independently of their own opinions and attitudes. It has since been claimed that this assumption was unjustified. Zavalloni and Cook (1965), for example, showed that anti-segregationist Americans judged statements opposing racial integration as more unfavourable to the Blacks than did the segregationists. This finding was according to prediction, and indicates the relevance of the judges' opinions. An unexpected finding was that the anti-segregationists judged the statements favourable to the Blacks as more favourable than did the segregationists. These unexpected findings are not unique, but were replicated by Sellitz, Edrich and Cook (1965).

Eiser's view is that these results can be explained in terms of the categorisation process. In his first study, Eiser claimed that the categorisation process was relevant in this kind of situation. He reasoned as follows. Confronted with a number of statements to judge, the subjects in Zavalloni's and Sellitz's experiments would classify them into two categories, the one including statements acceptable to them, the other statements unacceptable. This categorisation would then be reflected in judgment by the accentuation of the differences between the two classes, and of the similarities between statements classed together, in respect of a dimension correlated with the division of statements into acceptable and unacceptable with respect to their favourability toward the object of the attitude studied. This presupposes that the categorisation process is relevant whenever a subject is required to judge a series of statements. Accordingly, systematic category membership was superimposed on a series of statements to be judged. The same experiment was intended to test whether subjects favourably or unfavourably disposed toward the object of the attitude differed in their judgment.

The experiment was carried out in an English university.

The attitude studied was that toward the non-medical use of drugs. Subjects were presented with 64 statements concerning the use of drugs. They were asked to indicate to what extent they found each statement tolerant or permissive on a scale from 1 (extremely tolerant) to 11 (extremely intolerant). This corresponded to the task of Thurstone's judges. The measure of the attitude of the subjects was in terms of the degree of agreement or disagreement they expressed with the different statements. This enabled the subjects to be divided into a 'pro' and an 'anti' group. The main independent variable in the experimental situation was introduced by presenting the 32 most tolerant statements as coming from a paper called 'The Messenger' and the 32 most critical statements as coming from another paper called 'The Gazette'. The subjects were told that these were fictitious names, as the experimenter could not give the real names of the papers in case this might influence their judgments. In fact, the statements came from a wide variety of sources. In the control situation, there was no reference to papers, but the subjects had to judge the same statements.

The question is whether the statements which had been assigned to classes were judged differently from the statements which had not been so assigned; and whether this affected 'pro' and 'anti' subjects equally. Table 10 shows that both factors were important. When statements were classified, the differences between tolerant statements and intolerant statements were greater than when statements were not so classified. This confirms the main hypothesis. As far as the accentuation of intra-category similarities is concerned, i.e. the other aspect of the categorisation process, the findings do not allow any conclusion to be drawn. They tend to support the hypothesis, but at a statistically insignificant level. Both when statements are categorised and when they are not categorised, subjects who are 'pro' are more polarised than subjects who are 'anti'. The findings of Zavalloni and Cook are thus confirmed, in a different context and with fresh material, although the results were not explained.

Table 10. *Mean judgments of statements favourable and unfavourable to the free use of drugs*

Subjects	Statements	Without categorisation condition	With categorisation condition
Pro	Favourable	4.067	3.626
	Unfavourable	8.389	8.433
Anti	Favourable	4.131	3.594
	Unfavourable	7.731	8.076

SOURCE: Eiser, 1971.

Eiser's experiment therefore indicates that the categorisation of statements expressing attitudes did affect judgment, but did not explain how the attitude of the subjects affected the operation of this categorisation process. Why should segregationist subjects in the United States and subjects opposed to the use of drugs in Great Britain accentuate the differences between favourable and unfavourable statements less than other subjects? Eiser (1971, p. 2) has put forward one explanation. We have to distinguish between two factors: (1) the actual rating which the subjects give to the statements; (2) the values attached to the poles of the scale in terms of which the subjects evaluate the statements. When we take account of both these factors, we can see that the 'anti' subjects are in both cases in a peculiar kind of situation. They are being asked to classify the statements they accept in terms of the negative pole of the scale and to describe in terms of the positive pole those statements which they reject. This assumes that in the groups studied, it was regarded as undesirable to be hostile to Blacks or to be intolerant and prohibitive. If this interpretation of values is accepted, it is understandable that 'anti' subjects were more reluctant to give definite judgments than 'pro' subjects, who could react favourably to opinions they accepted and unfavourably to opinions they rejected.

Eiser and Stroebe further develop this interpretation, which was later to find experimental confirmation.

Suppose we asked a sample of American students to rate a set of statements concerning the Vietnam war along some such dimension as 'peace-loving – war-mongering'. One would suspect that subjects who were opponents of US policy in Vietnam would be quite happy to describe the kinds of opinions which they themselves would accept as 'peace-loving' and quite prepared to describe the positions they themselves would reject as 'war-mongering'. In their case, the approval and disapproval implied by the judgment scale terms would be consistent with their own acceptance and rejection of the items in the various regions of the scale. Supporters of US intervention, on the other hand, would be in the position of having to describe opinions which they themselves accepted as 'war-mongering' and those which they rejected as 'peace-loving'. If, on the other hand, the same statements had to be rated along some such scale as 'patriotic–unpatriotic', it would be the pro-war judges who could rate statements which they accepted as closer to the end of the scale with the more positive value connotations. It would seem plausible that in such a situation the pro-war judge would be more prepared than the anti-war judge to discriminate between the statements on a scale like 'patriotic–unpatriotic', whereas the anti-war judge would be more prepared than the pro-war judge to discriminate between the statements on a scale like 'peace-loving–war-mongering'. We might expect, therefore, that the pro-war judge would give more polarised ratings than the anti-war judge on the 'patriotic–unpatriotic' scale, whereas the anti-war judge would give more polarised ratings than the pro-war judge on the 'peace-loving–war-mongering' scale (Eiser and Stroebe, 1972, p. 153).

Two bipolar dimensions are therefore involved when subjects are asked to judge a series of expressions of opinion – acceptance or rejection of the content of these opinions and the value implications of the poles of the scale used. When the two sets of judgments correspond, they support one another. This is the case for the 'pro' subjects in the experiments concerned. When the two dimensions are at odds, as in the case of the 'contra' subjects in the same experiments, the effects tend to cancel one another out. An experiment therefore seemed called for to show that, in the case of the 'contra' subjects, there might also be accentuation of differences between accepted and rejected statements when the former were described in terms of the positive pole of the scale used and the latter in terms of the negative pole. Eiser proposed two such experiments. Thirty items, already used in the previous experiment, served as material for judgment in the first experiment (Eiser, 1973), designed to explain the asymmetry in the operation of the categorisation process when it concerns value-loaded social attitudes. In this experiment, subjects were not asked simply to describe the statements on a scale from tolerant to restrictive, but also on four other scales. The value implications of the poles of these scales varied. In the case of two of the scales (immoral–moral and decadent–respectable), the pole corresponding to tolerant became negative, while for the other two scales (liberal–authoritarian and broadmindedness–narrowmindedness), the value implications of the poles corresponded to those of the first scale. In this task, both the 'contra' subjects and the 'pro' subjects were in a situation in which for some scales there was correspondence between the evaluative implications of the poles and the acceptance or rejection of the content of the statements, while for other scales there was no such correspondence. It was predicted that, for each group of subjects, there should be more polarisation of judgment in the case of the 'concordant' scales than in the case of the 'discordant' scales; and this was indeed found to be the case. In the second experiment (Eiser and Mower White, 1974), similar results emerged with material consisting of statements in favour of or against the authority of adults, with adolescent subjects and different scales. Subjects more in favour of adult authority polarise more in their descriptions of opinion items on the scales such as 'co-operative–unco-operative' or 'patient–impatient', subjects who question this authority polarise more on the scales 'progressive–reactionary' or 'independent–dependent'.

We may draw the following provisional conclusion. A model of a psychological process is developed in the first place to account for the organisation of the perception of physical elements on which a systematic categorisation is superimposed. This model describes a process of differentiation which seems to reflect an important aspect of the relatively early development of sensory perception in the evolution of species. The process plays an orienting role in relation to the physical environment, via the objective links which exist between factors directly necessary to the organism and factors which are not thus directly necessary. The model also applies to the individual organisation of social experience. Elaborations of the process take account of modifications associated with the particular position of the individual in his social environment. By developing the model of the categorisation process, psychological experiments have undoubtedly provided us with an important instrument for explaining the adjustment of man to his physical and social environment.

This does not imply that research on the psychological process of categorisation is complete. We still require to give a more solid empirical basis to the hypotheses concerning its phylogenetic origins. The version of the process relevant to the accentuation of intra-category similarities also needs further exploration. Finally, it seems likely that, while the process orients the individual in his social environment, other modifications, such as those studied by Eiser, are also of importance. Like every process going on in a physical or social environment, it interacts with other processes. The study of such interaction is only beginning, and in the following chapter, we shall develop another example concerned with the experimental integration of convergence and categorisation.

There is yet another gap in the existing psychological research on categorisation. In this field, as in others, we lack empirical work on the sociogenic factors involved in the development of the process in the individual. Even if one accepts, as we do, that the origins of the process are phylogenetic, one must still try to discover how it emerges with the assimilation of social experience, in the course of individual development. Indeed, if the categorisation process is a psychological one, it is essential to study it at this level.

In the previous chapter, we saw that intergroup effects, in so far as they can be produced experimentally, may essentially represent a differentiation effect associated with category differentiation. We shall presently confirm that this is indeed so. If the categorisation process thus operates at both the psychological level and the social level, this must be because it constitutes a social psychological process representing a point of integration between the psychological and the sociological, and relates individual dynamics to social dynamics.

A SOCIAL PSYCHOLOGICAL PROCESS

The categorisation process not only enables the individual to organise his subjective experience of the social environment but also, and perhaps more importantly, constitutes a process by which social interaction is structured, differentiates among, and shapes individuals. This is possible because categorisation does not arise only from social levels of perception, judgment or evaluation, but also from social interaction. The process takes social change into account because it can account for differentiating behaviour. The process thus indicates a mode of integration of collective behaviour which transforms reality. Such transformations consist mainly of differentiations between social groups or categories. This is why from now on we shall refer to the process as category differentiation, thus indicating that the behaviours involved in social differentiation take place according to the categorisation process.

Epistemologically, the process of category differentiation certainly implies an isomorphism or structural analogy between individual and social reality. This will be made clear below. But just as we postulated above that social interaction had a causal influence on the development of cognitive integration in the individual, we now postulate the same for the process of category differentiation as it is reflected in individual actions. In this sense, a social psychological process is involved, which effectively integrates both changes affecting the individual and changes affecting the activity of individuals in common, as we shall now make clear.

We give below six propositions characterising the process of category differentiation. We shall later show that these propositions account for a large part of the intergroup effect as illustrated experimentally and described in the preceding chapter.

Description of the process of category differentiation

1. Differentiation of aspects of the social reality occurs in association with other differentiations relevant to the same reality, just as, according to the model provided by the categorisation process, perceptual differentiations occur in association with other perceived differentiations.

2. Category differentiation gives rise to behavioural, evaluative and representational differentiations.

3. Category differentiation takes place within the fields of behaviour, evaluation and representation as well as between these fields. Differentiation in one field may therefore be associated with differentiation in another field.

4. When there is differentiation at one of these three levels (behavioural, evaluative or representational) there is a tendency for corresponding differentiations to be made at the other levels.

5. Differentiation at the behavioural level has a stronger effect on the development of other differentiations than differentiation at the other two levels.

6. Differentiations produced by different social memberships, common to a number of individuals, associate individual differentiations with social differentiations. Category differentiation is therefore a social psychological process relating individual activities to social activities through intergroup evaluations and representations.

Experimental reinterpretations

The categorisation process model, which for Tajfel referred to a mode of understanding reality in the Kantian sense, now becomes, on the basis of the six propositions above, a model which takes account not only of social understanding but also and most significantly of a process of social transformation of reality. It thus particularly facilitates the integration of the experimental intergroup effects which we considered in the previous chapter, into a single theoretical framework. Such a reinterpretation of these findings illustrates the economy of the process of category differentiation, in terms of which we can explain a complex of very varied data.

The theoretical framework proposed by Sherif to account for intergroup effects was certainly one of the most coherent. It is therefore important to see how it fits in with the process of category differentiation.

Sherif's explanation was in terms of goals. The incompatibility of the goals of two groups led to phenomena such as hostile behaviour, unfavourable intergroup images, overvaluation of the product of one's own group and the restructuring of sociometric choices, while the introduction of one superordinate goal put an end to these forms of behaviour by bringing the two separated groups together again. These findings can be re-interpreted in terms of the category differentiation model. If we accept the notion that the creation of incompatibility with respect to goals implies differentiation at the behavioural level, the model predicts that such differentiation will be accompanied by differentiation at the representational level, at the evaluative level and in other forms of behaviour. The introduction of convergence at the behavioural level as effected in a superordinate goal should, on the other hand, reduce other forms of differentiation. This is what happened in the 'Robbers' Cave' experiment, which thus shows that differentiation or convergence at the behavioural level brings corresponding differentiation or convergence at the other levels.

The work of Blake and Mouton (1961, 1962a), which

demonstrates more specifically that groups in competition tend not to see what is common in their products, also illustrates the connection between differentiation at the behavioural level and differentiation at the cognitive, representational level.

It is not only competition, i.e. the attempt to implement incompatible goals, which leads groups in the direction of behavioural differentiation. It is sufficient if two groups are asked to carry out a task independently, as Ferguson and Kelley (1964) show, and as Sherif also found in the group formation phase of his first experiments, for various differentiations, both evaluative and sociometric, to appear between the two groups. Conflict is not necessary; separation at the behavioural level is sufficient for the appearance of differentiation at the level of evaluation and representation.

Several other experiments also show that interaction between competitive or just co-active groups does not have to end, for evaluative differentiations to begin to appear. In a situation similar to that of Ferguson and Kelley (1964), in which there was again no induction of competition, Rabbie and Wilkens (1971) noted that two groups asked to carry out identical tasks independently, already showed, even before carrying out the task, an evaluative bias in favour of their own group. Similar results appear in the case of anticipation of competitive interaction (Doise, 1969d). All the indications seem to be that the effects predicted by category differentiation are produced not only by behavioural divergence or separation, but also by the mere anticipation of these.

If differentiation at the behavioural level does indeed lead to differentiation at the other two levels, is the converse also true? We shall now consider some studies which manipulate differences at the evaluative and representational levels as independent variables. It is difficult to distinguish between these two levels, and we shall make no attempt to do so here.

Mannheim (1960) reports an experiment in which he manipulated the image of the 'other group', the members of which were said to be more or less intelligent and more or less satisfied with a hierarchical structure than the members of the membership group. The induction of these differences provoked more aggressive behaviour toward the other group. On the other hand, when similarities were induced, the groups behaved in a more co-operative way.

As far as linguistic family membership is concerned, Germans are closer to Austrians than are Italians. They also show more favourable attitudes to Austrians than to Italians. Starting from these existing relations, Mees (1974) similarly shows that in an experimental situation, German subjects show less aggressiveness toward an Austrian than toward an Italian. Moreover, different measures obtained in the same experiment indicate that aggressiveness toward foreigners is indeed a function of pre-existing less favourable attitudes toward them. There is therefore a connection between rejection at the attitude level and rejection at the behavioural level, which had not been shown in several previous experimental studies which controlled the variables involved less rigorously (see Mees, 1974, pp. 35ff).

An experiment very relevant for showing the effect which other forms of differentiation produce at the behavioural level is that of Billig and Tajfel (1973). This experiment shows that the categorisation of a population into two groups, even at random, heads or tails, is sufficient to induce discriminatory behaviour between the members of one's own group and those of the other group, even although this may diminish the absolute gains accruing to one's own group. The same experiment, however, also shows that the mere fact of having expressed similar or different aesthetic preferences in a previous experimental task, without there being any division into groups, is not enough to induce similar discrimination. This finding appears at first sight to be contrary to the proposed model, since different preferences do not lead to discrimination, whereas an arbitrary division into categories, without any genuine differences, does lead to discrimination. The reason is that the proposed model is relevant to *category* discrimination and it is only when group or class membership is real for the subjects that the process can operate. In the situation which involved only similarity, and in which Billig and Tajfel did not introduce membership of a group as a function of previous choices, the subjects apparently did not make such a categorisation either. This does not mean that simple objective similarities and differences which persist over time cannot lead to categorisation. We may refer here to the example of an area of Chicago where the colour of their houses is the only observable differentiating factor between inhabitants of the same socio-economic state. 'One portion of the sequence of buildings is red and the other is white. Arbitrary as this difference seems, it is a major cleavage in the area, and there is mutual opposition between the residents in the red buildings and those in the white' (Suttles, 1972, p. 28). It is scarcely surprising that the author who reported this observation developed a conception of the taxonomy of urban areas which shows similarities to the category differentiation model (ibid, p. 32).

In the experiment by Rabbie and Horwitz (1969), the lot of the experimental subjects was determined in different ways, depending on their memberships of two categories. Is such differentiation to be regarded as based on behaviour, evaluation or representations? In a way, it involves all three levels. It gives rise to fresh evaluative and sociometric discriminations which do not appear in the control groups, in which the differential labelling of the subjects had no significance for them and thus failed to activate the process of category differentiation.

As far as the effects of intergroup relations upon intra-group relations is concerned, it has been shown that these are reflected in an accentuation of the status hierarchy of the members of the group (Harvey, 1956) or in a return to orthodoxy (Deconchy, 1971). It is believed that status and power are the particularly salient factors in groups, and that the effect of accentuation of intra-group similarities is that subjects make primary reference to them in intergroup situations to increase the chances of mutual rapprochement. More directly, the accentuation of intra-group similarities has been confirmed in our experiment on polarisation in an intergroup situation (Doise, 1969a). When in this experiment the subjects were confronted with the appearance of another group, their judgments, made both individually and collectively, were less scattered than when there was no reference to the other group. Of the ten judgments which the subjects were required to make in this experiment, this effect occurred in nine cases in the individual situation and in eight cases in the group situation. This provides a further illustration of the fact that manipulation at the representational level can induce changes in accordance with the dynamic process of category differentiation. The effect of this dynamic process is also reflected in the more favourable sociometric status accorded to the extremists in the membership group when the other group is referred to.

The integration of different forms of differentiation, according to experimental findings, thus seems to develop as the category differentiation model indicates. Not only can this model accommodate Sherif's conceptual framework; its range is sufficiently great to integrate other theoretical conjectures concerning intergroup relations. The more recent analyses by Tajfel (1972), in terms of category identification, may virtually be assimilated by the model as they are, although this is not so for the explanation in terms of the need for identity as proposed by Turner (1975), which confines itself to the psychological aspect of what is a social psychological process. The model which we propose is a structural one. The transformations which it describes, however, cannot occur without dynamic processes which conform to the laws of the model. Avigdor (1953) and Wilson, Chun and Kayatani (1965), studying the selective and justificatory aspects of intergroup representations as a function of the interaction situation, work with this dynamic, structural concept. The asymmetrical aspect of this dynamic structure appears in the universal stereotype described by Campbell (1967) and in the work of Peabody (1968), which shows how qualities which are 'objectively' identical may be differently evaluated by members of the group and by non-members. The dynamics of the process become creative when, as in the experiments cited by Lemaine (1966), the situations are re-defined by the groups so as to initiate category differentiation.

A particularly appropriate intergroup situation for the study of the dynamics of category differentiation is that in which several category memberships are induced at the same time. This was the case in the experiment by Bass and Dunteman (1963), in which there was both membership of a group and an alliance between groups. Here, the allied group became a means of safeguarding the differentiation in favour of one's own group. Membership of several groups was also manipulated in our Grenoble experiment (Doise, 1969a). It may be remembered that French and German subjects were divided differentially into antagonistic groups. When national membership and membership of a temporary interest group coincided, intergroup discrimination was greater than when the two memberships were crossed. In the latter case, category differentiations acted in opposite directions and their effects tended to cancel one another. Such cross memberships probably partly explain the findings of Diab (1970). In the following chapter we shall return to the particular characteristics of category differentiation where cross categorisation is involved.

All the interpretations which we have advanced so far on the basis of the process of category differentiation are in a way *post hoc* interpretations. They enable us to invoke the principle of economy in favour of the model. The variety of findings which it can account for is greater than that of the main rival model, that of Sherif. But might this not be because the category differentiation model is too general in nature? This would indeed be the case if it allowed only *a posteriori* explanations. But after the model was constructed, fresh experiments were carried out to demonstrate in detail the way in which it works. In the following chapter we shall give an account of these experiments.

The conclusion which may be drawn from what we have said so far is only provisional. It is that one process can account for the way in which, in very different situations, a form of social organisation consisting of groups develops and affects the behaviour of individuals who, in their turn, in the process of interacting, confirm this form of organisation. In this way, the process of category differentiation constitutes a genuine social psychological process.

3

Recent experimental support

Experimental findings already well established provided the grounds on which, in the previous chapter, we were able to define and illustrate the operation of the category differentiation process. We shall now show how the process operates under other conditions, and indicate ways in which it functions, which have hitherto received little or no attention. However, our interest in increasing our knowledge of the workings of the categorisation process was not the only reason for this new series of studies of intergroup behaviour. They were also intended to indicate our position with regard to the issue of the validity of experimental studies, to which we have already referred. If this controversy does indeed reflect opposition between those who hold that experiment, as described in the preceding chapters, may contribute to the understanding of social reality, and those who think that such experimental situations are too artificial to tell us anything worthwhile about this social reality, it should be clear that we align ourselves with the former. It seems to us, however, that this kind of issue is fruitless because it is based on a false distinction between 'artificial' situations and 'natural' situations. The experimental situation is a real situation with real social actors. Indeed, we should hesitate to say that a 'laboratory' situation is less complex or simpler than a 'natural' situation. It is true that the experimental situation is designed to compare situations which vary only in certain respects, but one must equally simplify when one is concerned with situations outside the laboratory.

Understanding inevitably must be in terms of a limited

number of variables, and, as we have seen, at a specific level of analysis. Thus, it represents the simplified reconstruction of a complex and overdetermined aspect of reality.

Again, the experiment, although it emphasises certain aspects, nevertheless takes place within an overall structure of very closely woven relations. Any experiment takes place within and in relation to a social structure. The experimental subjects are also citizens and carry into the experimental situation a complex of ideas, norms, representations and evaluations. The researcher must therefore arrange the experimental situation so as to be reasonably sure that the factors significant for him are involved rather than other, less relevant factors. There is no such thing as a social vacuum. To try to create one, by artificially separating laboratory situations and natural situations, would be equivalent to entering a tunnel in which we could no longer distinguish the manipulated variables.

Our own view, which is that the experimental situation should be regarded as a genuinely social situation, and that the experimental subjects should be regarded as citizens, has important methodological implications. It implies that we should in every case consider the connections between the system of relations produced experimentally and the system of pre-existing relations, in order to reach a theoretical definition of the experimental situation. More specifically, when we study the relations between members of social groups, we must not forget the representations and norms which their social experience has previously instilled with regard to the customary form of relations. The particular interaction which the experimenter induces between members of these groups may coincide with, reinforce or be at odds with the habitual relations between these groups. The studies which we are going to report will in fact show that it is possible to take account of the structure of relations between groups established during social development, and to relate this to experimentally established relations; and that this is valuable in elucidating the dynamics of category differentiation.

The two-fold aim of illustrating the functioning of category differentiation and of putting the experimental procedure in its 'proper' place has neither been attempted nor attained in equal measure in all the experiments which will be described. Taken as a whole, however, the reports of these experiments should show that, in an experimental situation, behavioural, evaluative and representational differentiations tend to go together. Even when category memberships have been created experimentally, category differentiation only makes itself felt when it modifies pre-existing norms of behaviour and judgments.

INTERACTION AND MULTIPLE DIFFERENTIATION

The first experiments of Tajfel et al. (1971) on the discriminatory effects of category membership had just been published, when in July 1971 we managed to organise a working group on the relations between groups, with different researchers taking part. The first concern of the group was with the generality of the findings of Tajfel and his collaborators. The question was whether the same results would be found in a different country (West Germany), or with older subjects (recruits to the German Forces, who had completed their secondary school studies). Would the same norms as those governing the behaviour of English pupils also be found to govern the experimental behaviour of German soldiers? The results of Tajfel's experiment showed that his subjects followed at least two strategies, one designed to realise a positive difference in favour of the members of the membership category, and one which would prevent them from dissociating themselves too far from an equitable division between the members of the two categories. It was as if the Bristol subjects had brought two norms into the experimental situation. We were able, with the collaboration of Billig and Royser (unpublished) to show more directly the existence of these two norms. Several days after they had taken part in a Tajfel-type experiment, a sample of subjects was invited to explain the decisions taken on different matrices. About half of the sample justified their decision on the grounds that gains should be shared fairly; and half argued that the members of their own group should get special benefit. The same subjects often put forward both arguments, e.g. 'You must be "fair", but to give a little more to your own group isn't "unfair".'

It seems reasonable therefore, to suppose that similar norms applied to the behaviour of the German subjects. A kind of egalitarianism was the norm for soldiers of the same rank in an army claimed to be democratic. At the same time, however, there was written on the walls of their barracks, 'Besser wie die Andern' (We are better than them). Our experiment was basically intended to see whether the interplay between 'egalitarianism' and 'positive differentiation' would be reflected at the level of experimental behaviour.

The main aim of the Constance group was, however, more specific. It was chiefly concerned with explaining how the process of category differentiation intervened at different levels in the experimental production of discrimination. We wished to show that the process intervened in a dynamic way at the representational evaluative level. Tajfel and his collaborators induced their subjects to feel that they belonged to different categories and studied the effect of this at the level of reward-oriented behaviour. Our model predicts that variations at the behavioural level will also be reflected at the representational level, i.e. that the inducing of divergence in behaviour will accentuate differences or create fresh differentiation at the representational and evaluative level. It was therefore decided to study the effect of inducing differential category membership, by means similar to those used by Tajfel, at the representational and evaluative level, in a situation in which the subjects would not be required to take decisions concerning one another (control condition) and in situations in which they would have to take such decisions (experimental conditions). In order to study the integration between behaviour and representations, convergence or divergence of interests for a more or less valuable prize were manipulated in the experimental situations. The main hypothesis was that the introduction of competition for a valuable prize would be accompanied by more marked differentiation both at the evaluative level and at the level of more objective representations. In a way, this was tantamount to predicting the intervention of a circular causal process; differentiations at the representational level favour the appearance of divergent forms of behaviour, which in their turn favour the appearance of new differentiations at the representational level.

The experiment was carried out with the collaboration of 151 recruits to the West German Army. It was presented to them as being concerned with problems of decision-making. In the first part of the experiment, four groups of 30 subjects and one group of 31 subjects were asked to give their aesthetic preferences for each of a series of photographs of biological cells taken with the aid of an electron-microscope. Next, supposedly on the basis of an examination of the choices expressed, the subjects were in each case divided into two groups, group X and group Y. They were told individually which group they belonged to, so that they would not know which of their comrades belonged to their own category and which to the other.

In the second part of the experiment, the members of the four experimental groups were told that the experimenter had a sum of money which the subjects could share among themselves, the experiment still being on decision-making. They had to do this by using matrices of the kind used by Tajfel et. al. (1971), one of which (that opposing maximal gain to one's own group and to the other group) was presented and explained to them. At this point, the experimental variations were introduced, as follows. Half of the experimental subjects (competition condition, $N = 60$) were instructed to gain as much money as possible for their own group; this money had to be shared fairly among the members of the group after the experiment. The other half of the experimental subjects (co-operation condition, $N = 60$) were instructed to gain as much as possible for the two groups together; the total amount gained then had to be shared fairly among all the members of both groups X and Y. For each of these experimental conditions, on each trial, half of the subjects were told that each participant could gain between half a (Deutsch) mark and a mark (low reward condition), the others that they could gain at least five marks, and could easily gain ten marks (high reward condition). For the control condition (N = 31), no expectation of mutual remuneration was introduced after the division of the subjects into the two groups X and Y.

In the following phase of the experiment, which for the experimental groups preceded the decision-making with the matrices, the subjects were all asked how they pictured to themselves, first the members of their own group and then the members of the other group. To do so, they were given 24 seven-point bipolar scales. One of these scales was intended to control for the effect of the instructions (co-operative–competitive), 19 others had explicitly evaluative poles such as friendly–hostile, generous–mean, and just–unjust; the four remaining scales were concerned with more explicitly objective traits, fair–dark, large–small, fat–thin and active–quiet.

In the control condition, the experiment ended at that point; in the experimental conditions, it continued with the decision-making based on the matrices. For a detailed description of these matrices see Dann and Doise (1974). We reported there that the co-operation–competition manipulation was reflected in the decisions of the subjects at a very significant level. We also found that the introduction of a more valuable reward in no way prevented the subjects from reducing their absolute gain in value terms in order to establish a positive differentiation with respect to the members of the other group in the competitive condition. On the contrary, the increase in the value of the reward was accompanied by an intensification of the attempt to establish a positive differentiation.

These findings, like those obtained with the co-operation–competition scale, not only demonstrate the validity of our experimental manipulation, but also confirm the 'Tajfel' effect in modified conditions and with different subjects. But what about the effect of category differentiation at the level of evaluative and more objective representations? Our results are given in Table 11.

Table 11. *Mean differences between descriptions by members, of their own group and of the other group*

	Control condition	Competition		Co-operation	
		High prize	Low prize	High prize	Low prize
19 'evaluative' traits	9.87	19.70 (2.60)^x	13.43 (0.94)	14.60 (1.25)	17.48 (1.96)
4 'objective' traits	5.10	8.33 (2.68)^x	7.43 1.93	7.10 1.66	6.25 0.94

The values of t in Dunnet's test are given in parentheses, for the comparison with the control group. $x = p < 0.05$.

Let us note first of all that, on the 19 evaluative scales, a difference in favour of the membership group was already present in significant measure in the control group. As expected, this difference became significantly more important when there was competition for the high reward. This finding confirms the effect of behavioural divergence at the evaluative level, even when the behavioural divergence is only anticipated. When representations have a more obvious objective connotation, the situation where there is competition for a high reward is also associated with a significantly greater degree of differentiation than the control situation.

One problem remains. Although the condition of competition for a high reward differs significantly in the expected direction from the control condition, the experimental conditions do not differ significantly from one another. More experiments are therefore called for, in which co-operation and competition are manipulated more meaningfully by using more suitable measuring instruments, before we can confirm that behavioural divergence and convergence are indeed accompanied by corresponding changes at the representational and evaluative level. The following research provides such confirmation.

THE DYNAMICS OF A MASCULINE IDEOLOGY

The following experiment, carried out with the collaboration of Weinberger, was again intended to confirm that behavioural divergence and convergence bring divergence or convergence at the representational level as well. A more detailed account of this experiment has been given by Doise and Weinberger (1972–3). If there is a stereotype supported by well-established, though disputed, reports in our society, it is that which men have created of women; on the content of this stereotype, see Rocheblave-Spenlé (1964) and Chombart de Lauwe, Huguet, Perroy and Bisseret (1967). In accordance with the points of view outlined in the introduction to this chapter, we wished to show that even representations involving an ancient 'natural division' (Moscovici, 1972) could be modified in a way predictable by the category differentiation process model.

There were three main experimental conditions in this research: one co-operative, intended to study the effect of behavioural convergence on the representations which men in this situation formed of their female partners; one of induced competition, intended to study the effect on these same representations exerted by divergence introduced specifically at the level of behavioural intentions; and one of spontaneous competition where the two parties simply had to carry out a task in one another's presence, a situation which should lead spontaneously to competition in Turner's sense (1975), and stimulate representations similar to those in the induced competition situation.

In each of these three conditions, another variable was also manipulated. In each trial, one boy was confronted with one girl (individual encounter situation), and pairs of boys were confronted with pairs of girls (group encounter situation).

Intuitively, it was felt that interaction between two pairs represents more of an intergroup situation than interaction between two persons. The analysis in terms of possibility of convergence, as carried out in the case of the following experiment, will confirm this hypothesis, which had indeed already been confirmed by other investigators (Dustin and Davis, 1970). We therefore predicted that competitive group interaction would accentuate the evaluative sexual representations more than individual competitive interaction. The subjects in this experiment were 90 boys, volunteers, who were students at a commercial studies college in Paris. They took part in the experiment along with a female collaborator of the experimenter, who was always the same person in the individual situation. In the group situations, this collaborator was backed up by another. These collaborators were presented as students who had volunteered to participate in the experiment. Two identical sets of apparatus, said to be concerned with 'spatial co-ordination' were placed on each side of a table, in front of the student and the female collaborator, or in front of the two students and the two collaborators. A cursor was placed on each apparatus, in the middle. The task of the subjects was to push it to one end, and then to move it between the two extremities. The cursor could be worked by one individual or by two persons. In the group encounter situation, the boys manipulated one piece of apparatus together, while the girls manipulated the other.

When the subjects were installed, the experimenter distributed to each one an instruction sheet which began,

In this laboratory, we are interested in the behaviour of individuals in carrying out a spatial co-ordination task. There are two kinds of things we are interested in: (1) knowing what kind of picture of another person, and of one's self we form (in the two to two situation, what kind of picture we form of others and of ourselves) in the carrying out of a task; (2) recording the different strategies used in this kind of task. Here is what you have to do: describe, without talking to one another, how you think you would behave, and how the other person would behave (in the two to two situation, how you think you would both behave, and how you think the other two persons would behave), by answering 'Yes' or 'No' opposite the adjectives on the lists supplied.

The rest of the instructions varied according to the nature of the interaction. In the co-operation conditions, it was announced that the subjects had to decide together (in the two to two situation, all four together) the best strategy for this kind of task so that their result could be compared with that of other groups.

In the induced competition conditions, they were asked to solve the problem as quickly as possible, before the other person or the other pair. In the spontaneous competition conditions, they were simply asked to carry out the task. Once the instructions were read, each subject had to respond to two identical lists of adjectives, the first of which was headed 'Description of your own behaviour' (individual condition) or 'Description of your common behaviour' (group condition). The second was headed 'Description of the behaviour of the other person' or 'Description of the behaviour of the other two people'. The adjectives which made up these lists are given in Table 12. Table 12 also indicates whether other students judged these traits as specifically masculine (M) or feminine (F), as positive (+) or negative (−). It may be noted that our judges considered 12 qualities masculine, 12 feminine, 15 positive and 17 negative.

On the basis of the responses to these lists, four scores were calculated: (1) The index of differentiation, i.e. the sum of all the times a subject gave different responses on the two lists; (2) the evaluative index, which reflects the difference between the number of positive and negative qualities to which a subject responded affirmatively on one list; (3) the index of femininity, which gives the number of feminine traits which a subject checked on a list; (4) the index of masculinity, which gives the number of masculine traits to which a subject responded affirmatively.

These scores reflect different, mutually interrelated, aspects of an ideological representation. But the question is

Table 12. *List of qualities used in their experiment by Doise and Weinberger*

active	M+	individualistic	−
ambitious	−	intelligent	+
authoritarian	M−	intuitive	F
curious	F+	clumsy	−
narrow-minded	−	methodical	M+
abrupt	M−	nervous	−
calm	+	passive	F−
temperamental	F−	patient	+
systematic	+	persevering	+
determined	M+	practical	+
submissive	F	prudent	+
animated	−	reasonable	M
firm	M	thoughtful	M+
clever	+	rigid	M−
hesitant	F−	risk-taking	M−
imaginative	F	cunning	F
impatient	−	sensitive	F
impulsive	F−	serious	M+
incoherent	F−	self-assured	M+
flighty	F−		

SOURCE: Doise and Weinberger, 1972–3.

whether they behaved in accordance with the interaction predicted by the category differentiation process model. Let us examine the following analyses.

The differentiations between the representations which the subjects form of the two parties in interaction vary according to the variations in the nature of the interaction. Incompatibility built into the nature of the interaction itself leads to the projection of further divergences at the representational level, and compatibility at the behavioural level leads to the projection of more similarities at the representational level. Table 13 gives the means for the index of differentiation and proves our point in the case of both individual and group conditions. The other scores however suggest that the differentiations in the individual conditions are not the same as in the group conditions. Contrary to the previous figures, these vary between conditions on an evaluative and sexual dimension.

Table 13. *Mean differentiation indices*

Experimental conditions	Situation 1 to 1	Situation 2 to 2
Co-operation	10.50	7.70
Induced competition	13.50	13.55
Spontaneous competition	13.80	11.40

Difference between co-operation condition and competition conditions: $F = 16.966$, d.f. $= 1, 54$, $p < 0.001$.

The study of the evaluative index shows in fact that competitive interaction affects attributions differently in individual and group situations. In the latter, there is more evaluative discrimination when spontaneous or induced competition produces incompatibility at the behavioural level. When there is individual competition, the evaluative bias is in the opposite direction. In their observations on the evaluation of products under conditions of individual and group competition, Dustin and Davis (1970) report comparable findings.

To admit that one possesses qualities judged to be typical of another category constitutes a form of approach to this category, at the representational level. To deny these qualities in oneself, while attributing them to members of the other category represents a form of estrangement at the representational level. We shall therefore examine how the attribution of feminine qualities varies across the different experimental conditions. It may be noted first that, although our index is not wholly independent of the index of evaluative discrimination (it contains 7 of the 32 evaluative qualities), it nevertheless contains 5 non-evaluative qualities. Therefore we should not expect results identical to those previously discussed. However, when competition is anticipated, the fact that the other party belongs to the feminine category is significantly more accentuated in the case of group encounters than in the case of individual encounters. When co-operation is anticipated, such a difference does not occur.

Table 14. *Mean indices of evaluation*

Experimental conditions	Situation 1 to 1		Situation 2 to 2	
	Judgment of self	Judgment of others	Judgment of self	Judgment of others
Co-operation	8.00	8.80	9.45	9.35
Induced competition	2.50	7.70	6.50	4.90
Spontaneous competition	4.30	6.50	9.50	4.70

Values of F for the two competitive conditions in relation to the interaction between situations 1 to 1, 2 to 2 and target persons: 9.54 and 10.11; d.f. = 1, 54; $p < 0.01$.

The attribution of masculine traits follows more or less the same pattern for self and for other, for one's own pair and for the other pair, across the different experimental conditions. The results for the masculinity index thus do not confirm the main hypotheses of the research. They show no significant difference, although it is the other party who, in the competitive and group conditions, seems to receive the smaller number of qualities typical of the category membership of our male subjects.

Let us summarise our findings. When there is group interaction, the divisions introduced by an anticipated conflict of interest intensify existing social divisions. When there is interaction between individuals, things look as though these divisions were easily obscured. This might be because the subjects hesitate to define themselves in terms of their membership category in this situation. The last studies to be reported in this chapter will show that the difference between the two situations is not necessarily due to the fact that the object of the judgments in these encounters changes.

Table 15. *Mean femininity indices*

Experimental conditions	Situation 1 to 1		Situation 2 to 2	
	Judgments of self	Judgments of others	Judgments of self	Judgments of others
Co-coperation	5.50	5.60	5.75	5.75
Induced competition	7.00	5.80	5.85	7.00
Spontaneous competition	6.80	6.30	5.50	7.15

Values of F for the two competitive conditions in relation to the interaction between situations 1 to 1, 2 to 2 and target persons: 5.87 and 4.91; d.f. $= 1, 54$; $p < 0.05$.

Table 16. *Mean masculinity indices*

Experimental conditions	Situation 1 to 1		Situation 2 to 2	
	Judgments of self	Judgments of others	Judgments of self	Judgments of others
Co-operation	6.80	6.40	6.70	6.80
Induced competition	7.60	7.10	6.55	6.15
Spontaneous competition	7.50	7.40	6.90	6.20

THE ASYMMETRICAL FUNCTIONING OF THE PROCESS

The preceding study immersed the process of category differentiation in social reality. The experiment which we shall now describe does so even more completely by studying its operation in the representatives of two groups, without the intervention of collaborators. The two groups concerned occupied well defined positions in their social system, as a result of which we shall describe certain modifications in the operation of the process.

The general aim of the experiment was to study the representations which members form of their own group and of another group in conditions in which category differentiation can easily occur and in conditions in which it occurs less readily. Suppose that, in an experimental situation, we ask members of a pre-existing group to make judgments of their own group. For some of them (condition 1), that is all we ask at the beginning of the experiment. But after the end of this preliminary task, we ask them to describe another group. For others (condition 2) we tell them at the beginning that they will also have to describe another group using the same scales. These two experimental conditions, in which members of the other group are never actually present, are different. In condition 2, the categorisation can have effect from the very beginning, while in condition 1, when the description of the membership group is made, there is no reference to any other group, and hence no differentiation process within a well-defined frame of reference.

Suppose now that we ask the members of the same groups for the same descriptions, but with both groups present together. One might justifiably think that the category differentiation process would operate evenly to start with, but not in the same way when there was an individual encounter between a member of each group (condition 3) and when there was a group encounter with at least two members in each group (condition 4). In both cases, we have a situation involving judgment in the presence of others. Studies on judgments under conditions of co-presence, or on judgments made after exchange of information or after discussion, indicate that convergence comes about rather easily. Sometimes there is convergence toward a moderate position, sometimes toward an extreme position (Doise and Moscovici, 1973; Moscovici and Doise, 1974), or toward two extreme and opposed positions (see the effects of bipolarisation observed by Mugny, 1974, and Paicheler, 1974). In the case of an individual encounter between two individuals belonging to different groups and making judgments on these groups, the effect of convergence with regard to the other may offset the effect of category differentiation. This is no longer necessarily the case when, in a group encounter situation, the convergence effect may operate among the members of a group. In this situation, the effect of convergence will be to strengthen the bonds between members of the same group compared with members of different groups. This leaves category differentiation free to produce a certain degree of bipolarisation.

Such encounters between members of two social groups, however, do not take place in a sociological vacuum. The subjects in these groups reproduce and transform pre-existing representations. The groups who took part in our own experiment were apprentices in Geneva, the others, college students in the same city. It is obvious that the latter occupied a relatively privileged position in current Swiss society. Such a factor inevitably plays a part in the operation of the social psychological processes to which we have been referring, as we shall now show.

We can fairly safely start from a model which involves both an 'ethnocentric' and a 'sociological' dimension in the situations studied. By an ethnocentric dimension, we mean a dimension in terms of which the members of a group readily tend to regard the members of their group more favourably, and to interpret social reality with a positive bias toward their own group. By a sociological dimension, we mean the kind of constraint which every society constructs and imposes more or less successfully on the bulk of its members. It places the different groups in a social system in relation to one another.

Although the ethnocentric and sociological dimensions may be relevant to the groups with which we are concerned, it does not follow that these groups are equally affected by those variables. In the case of the college students, the membership group and the 'other' group were similarly rated on both dimensions; the membership group was in each case closer to the positive pole than the 'other' group. This was not the case for the apprentices. For them, the membership group was nearer to the positive pole on the ethnocentric dimension, but the other group was nearer to the positive pole on the sociological dimension. This has important implications for the operation of the category differentiation process. Its manipulation should certainly be of more unambiguous significance for college students than for apprentices. For the former, the category differentiation process should operate in the same direction for both dimensions, while for the apprentices it should operate in opposing directions. For the apprentices, the sociological factor should operate against ethnocentric overvaluation. Let us now summarise these considerations in the form of experimental predictions.

1. When members of a group are asked to describe their own group without reference being made to another group, and then to describe another group (condition 1) the difference between the two descriptions will be less significant than when reference is made to the other group from the start (condition 2).

2. In the case of an actual, individual encounter between two individuals belonging to different groups (condition 3), the difference between the descriptions which they give of the two groups will be less significant than in the case of symbolic encounter (condition 2).

3. In the case of an encounter of several individuals belonging to one group and several individuals belonging to another group (condition 4), the difference between the descriptions of the two groups will be more significant than in the case of individual encounter (condition 3).

4. The effect of the different encounter conditions will not be the same for members of a relatively privileged social group as for members of a less privileged group. The latter will react to the various experimental manipulations in ways which vary more among themselves.

The experiment was carried out with the participation of 105 subjects, of whom 56 were college students and 49 were apprentices in Geneva.

The experimental material was developed on the basis of a content analysis of fifteen interviews with apprentices and students. Twelve items concerned with typical qualities of apprentices and students were kept to form the experimental questionnaire. Of these twelve items, six were clearly considered by a sample group of 45 students and apprentices to have a content which was 'well-viewed' (two items) or 'poorly viewed' (four items). Our statistical analysis is based on these six items, which we shall reproduce here. The subjects had six possible responses – strongly disagree, disagree, inclined to disagree, inclined to agree, agree, strongly agree. These responses were scored respectively -3, -2, -1, $+1$, $+2$, $+3$ for the favourable items (items 5 and 12), the signs being reversed for the other items (items 1, 4, 6 and 10). The other six items concerned qualities which were less clearly evaluated. Each subject in the different experimental conditions had first to answer the items as applying to his own group, and then as applying to the other group. According to the circumstances, therefore, the dots in the statements below were replaced by the word 'apprentices' or the word 'students'.

The items used in the analysis of results were as follows.

Positively valued content

1. ....like the theatre.
2. ....are proud of being................

Negatively valued content

1. ....would rather talk about what goes on around them than about society in general.
2. Even if they have the necessary material, doing odd jobs presents practical difficulties for................
3. ....find difficulty in expressing themselves.
4. ....don't take much interest in world affairs.

The following are examples of items which appeared less valid and were not retained in the analysis.

1. The financial resources of................mean that they can easily get the equipment for skiing.
2. ....tend to marry between the ages of 20 and 22 years.

The different encounter situations were arranged as follows. In condition 1, 13 apprentices and 16 students, without any previous introduction, answered the two questionnaires at the beginning of a class hour. They were not told, when they answered the questionnaire for their own group, that they would later be asked to respond to the questionnaire as referring to the other group. In condition 2, when there was reference to the other group, 12 apprentices and 16 students were told, to start with, that they would also have to answer the same questionnaire in respect of the other group. In these two conditions, the questionnaires were administered to the students and apprentices in different places, as they attended classes in different schools.

In condition 3, an apprentice and a student, introduced to one another by the experimenter, first of all answered the two questionnaires individually. They then discussed together before answering a second time (there were eight apprentices and eight students). In condition 4, the procedure was the same as for condition 3, but the encounter was between two apprentices and two students (in all, 16 apprentices and 16 students).

Let us now look at the results. To isolate the effect of reference to the out-group, we shall first look at the description which members give of their own group in condition 1. For both groups, the intra-group description is not particularly favourable. Their responses indicate that they do not feel significantly more positive than negative towards their group. A comparison of this description of their membership group and the description which they later give of the other group, indicates no significant difference. On the other hand, for both groups, the descriptions of the other group are actually more favourable than the descriptions of the membership group, although this difference is not statistically significant (Table 17).

When the other group is referred to from the start, the subjects do not hesitate to present a favourable image of their own group. Moreover, the students now significantly overvalue their own group. For them, the differentiation in

Table 17. *Mean evaluation of 'membership group' and 'other group' recorded in different conditions of meeting*

		Subjects							
		Apprentices				Students			
			Evaluation of				Evaluation of		
Experimental conditions	N	Own group	Other group	Diff.	N	Own group	Other group	Diff.	
Without meeting									
Without reference	13	2.85 (1.80)	5.85 (3.06)	−3.00a (1.17)	16	0.38 (0.37)	0.94 (0.85)	−0.56e (0.36)	
With reference	12	4.50 (2.75)	3.25 (2.26)	+1.25b (0.52)	16	5.50 (6.96)	−0.75 (0.66)	+6.25 (4.86)f	
Condition 1 to 1									
Before discussion	8	3.88 (2.30)	7.50 (6.12)	−3.63c (3.45)	8	3.88 (2.22)	3.38 (2.83)	+0.50g (0.31)	
After discussion	8	0.13 (0.05)	5.25 (3.19)	−5.12d (3.10)	8	4.50 (2.83)	1.75 (1.04)	+2.75h (2.08)	
Condition 2 to 2									
Before discussion	16	2.94 (1.87)	6.88 (5.45)	−3.94 (3.14)	16	6.25 (5.19)	1.44 (1.40)	+4.81 (2.95)	
After discussion	16	4.56 (3.56)	6.56 (8.92)	−2.00 (1.62)	16	6.88 (7.62)	2.50 (2.75)	+4.38 (3.53)	

In parentheses are given the values of t in respect of the null hypothesis.

Values of t for different comparisons: a and b, 1.21; b and c, 1.58; b and d, 1.96 ($p < 0.04$, one-tailed test); e and f, 3.38 ($p < 0.01$); f and g, 2.68 ($p < 0.02$); f and h, 1.71 ($p < 0.05$, one-tailed test).

Significant values of F for an analysis of variance on conditions 1 to 1 and 2 to 2: difference between apprentices and students 43.92, d.f. = 1, 28, $p < 0.001$; difference between condition 1 to 1 and condition 2 to 2 4.57, d.f. 1, 28, $p < 0.025$.

Table 18. *Mean indices of central tendency of responses to the group membership questionaire*

Experimental conditions	Apprentices	Students
Without meeting		
Without reference	2.85	2.69a
With reference	2.67b	3.81c
Condition 1 to 1		
Before discussion	3.50	4.25
After discussion	3.00	3.88
Condition 2 to 2		
Before discussion	2.19	3.25
After discussion	3.44	4.19

t, for the differences, for unmatched sampled: *a* and *c*, 2.38 ($p < 0.05$); *b* and *c*, 2.74 ($p < 0.02$).

Significant *F*s for the analysis of variance for conditions 1 to 1, 2 to 2, apprentices and students: 7.79, d.f. = 1, 28, $p < 0.01$; 1 to 1, 2 to 2 × before–after: 8.89, d.f. = 1, 28, $p < 0.01$.

The index of central tendency varies from o to 6 and indicates the number of items for which the subjects have given a response coinciding with one of the two values within which occurred the mean of the responses of all the subjects belonging to the subject's group in the same experimental condition.

favour of their own group is positive and significantly different from the findings in the preceding condition. This tendency is less marked in the case of the apprentices. The experimental manipulation seems to mean something different for different members of this group. Some express positive differentiation, others yield to the pressure of the sociological factors which put their group at a disadvantage. This explanation would seem reasonable in the light of the index of central tendency (Table 18); this index is not appreciably higher for the apprentices in the case of symbolic encounter, but is so for the students. For the students, the cumulative effect of the experimental induction and of the nature of the representations results in a 'homogenising' of their responses. The situation is defined in the same way for everyone. This is not so in the case of the apprentices, and the conflict between experimental induction and the nature of their representations is manifested in a wider range of responses compared with the responses of the students.

Let us now look at the effect of actual encounter. Does actual individual encounter have a different effect from symbolic encounter? All the representations given before discussion, both with respect to the membership group and with respect to the other group are positive. In the case of the students, there is no longer any discrimination in favour of their own group; in the case of apprentices, there is actually a bias in favour of the other group. Concessions with regard to the other group are therefore significant in this situation. Discussion strengthens this tendency even further in the case of the apprentices, while in the case of the students, who confront 'other' from a position of strength, discrimination in favour of their own group tends to reappear after discussion.

In comparing the overall effect of intergroup encounter with the overall effect of individual encounter, before and after discussion, for the two groups of subjects, we find that the difference between the images of the two groups becomes more positive or less negative. This confirms our third hypothesis. Students again consider their own group definitely more favourably than the other group. The intergroup rapprochement observed in individual encounter gives way, as predicted, to category differentiation. But the apprentices still admit the superiority of the other group, more significantly before discussion, less clearly after discussion.

The study of the index of central tendency throws fresh light on what takes place in actual encounters. To begin with, the students give less varied responses among themselves than the apprentices. Next, the effect of convergence of responses on the part of the members of one's own group varies according to whether individual or group encounter is involved. In the case of individual encounter, there is a large implicit consensus in the responses between members of the same group. This agreement becomes less after discussion with a member of the other group. Discussion between individuals of different groups therefore lessens the effect of intra-group homogeneity. This does not happen during a collective encounter where discussion enhances intra-group homogeneity. This is precisely what we hypothesised.

To conclude, the combination of the notions presented by the category differentiation model with those concerned with group judgments and those relevant to the sociological positions of the interacting groups, has enabled us to predict the development of their representations in various experimental situations. The verification of our predictions illustrates the asymmetrical operation of differentiation. The following experiment is designed to show that, in certain situations, the effect of two dimensions of categorisation can be to offset one another.

THE EFFECTS OF CROSS MEMBERSHIPS

Experimentation which is carried out within a web of existing social relations is neither more nor less artificial than other situations. It may be admitted that the experimental situation, in so far as it is a temporary one, often creates temporary effects which are quickly absorbed by more important social determinants. We shall indeed show that this is so in the present experiment. Nevertheless, although effects may be temporary, the dynamics of an experimental situation function according to the laws of processes which have a degree of generality which goes beyond the situation under investigation. We shall once again demonstrate that this is indeed the case.

First of all, let us describe the specific dynamics of the category differentiation process with which our research, carried out with Deschamps (1975), was concerned. The conceptualisation of these dynamic processes was based on certain ideas taken from anthropology. A distinction between 'pyramidal–segmentary' structures and 'crosscutting' structures has been made by a number of anthropologists referred to by LeVine and Campbell (1972). Let us note first of all certain characteristics of the pyramidal–segmentary structure, which is

based on a virtually universal characteristic of societies: the membership of the individual in groups that are, in turn, segments of larger collectivities, so that each individual can correctly regard himself as a member of several units increasing in scope and inclusiveness up to the 'total society' itself. In any such pyramid of membership units, the individual must have a way of organizing these several claims that multiple membership makes on him, and he usually has a way of ranking his loyalties to groups at different levels. In examining the pyramidal type of loyalty structure, we are confronted with another universal attribute of group membership: that persons define themselves as group members by opposition or contrast to other groups, so that in order to identify himself to another, a person selects from his multiple memberships a group that will serve to distinguish him from members of other coeval groups at the level in the pyramid that he believes the person he is addressing has in mind. (ibid, pp. 43–5).

And the authors cite Evans-Pritchard (1940, p. 136).

If one meets an Englishman in Germany and asks him where his home is, he may reply that it is England. If one meets the same man in London and asks him the same question he will tell one that his home is in Oxfordshire, whereas if one meets him in that county he will tell one the name of the town or village in which he lives. If questioned in his town or village he will mention his particular street, and if questioned in his street he will indicate his house.

The characteristics of a pyramidal–segmentary structure have been particularly studied with regard to military loyalties. They allow hostility between sub-groups to be absorbed when the group including these sub-groups confronts another group at its own level. In this field, cross-cutting structures have the following properties.

1. Each male individual in the society owes military loyalty, or a more vaguely defined primary loyalty that involves defence under emergency conditions, to more than one group.

2. One of the groups to which he owes loyalty is his local group, to which he is bound not only by common residence but also by the common interests and co-operative activities which result from

common residence; the other is a group (based on common descent or age) whose members are dispersed over several local groups, each of which is a possible autonomous military unit.

3. No clear ranking of these two or more loyalties exists, so that when they make contradictory demands on the individual, he is disposed to find a novel way of satisfying the two or more groups instead of being disloyal to one of them (LeVine and Campbell, 1972, p. 47).

Ethnological observations show that a crosscutting structure, based on multiple memberships which hold across one another's boundaries, reduces the confrontations between the constituent parts of a society. It can readily be seen how marriage conventions can create one or the other type of society. A class which, in Jaulin's terminology (1973), refers to itself as 'one's own people' and consists of all those people like himself whom the individual may not marry, may become crossed with a class of 'other people' from which the individual may take a wife. Such a crossing of two groups may come about through cohabitation in collective houses, and represents a factor making for equilibrium and harmony.

If the basic social unit is a group in which one's own people and other people are bound together and 'intermixed', the other cannot be thought of negatively as non-self, but must be thought of first in a positive way, as being complementary. No doubt strictly, according to marriage regulations, this other may be regarded as non-self, but from the point of view of social order and functional human unity, whether we are concerned with questions of residence or with a core of forces varying in nature between civilisations – this other must be a necessary part of self (Jaulin, 1973, p. 306).

These ideas, which have been developed by anthropologists, may readily be integrated into the category differentiation model. Let us imagine a simple case of crossing of category memberships. Experimental subjects belong to one of two categories according to the criterion of sex: they are boys or girls. But according to another criterion, they also belong to one of two different categories, a 'red' and a 'blue' experimental group. Suppose we now cross the group memberships so that each group of boys or girls is composed of one half 'red' and one half 'blue', and that each group of 'blues' or 'reds' is composed of one half boys and one half girls. For each of the subjects, one half of the members of a membership category will belong to a different category from his or her own in terms of a different criterion.

How should the category differentiation process work in this kind of situation if both category memberships are made relevant for the subjects? There should be accentuation of both differences between the two sex categories and differences between the experimental categories. At the same time, there should be accentuation of differences within each category, since this category is composed of two categories which differ according to the other criterion. But according to the same process, there should also be accentuation of similarities within any category and with one part of the members of the other category. There should therefore be a conflict between accentuation of differences and accentuation of similarities within each category and between opposing categories. It may therefore be predicted that in this case opposing effects weaken the operation of category differentiation. We shall try to provide experimental proof that this is so.

The reduction in differentiation should, however, be limited. It should affect only those qualities which are relevant to the experimental situation. This is not simply an experimental artefact. Other situations which are not simply temporary and which are closely integrated within a social structure, do not necessarily have unlimited influence upon the category representations of those who originate them. Field studies show that the structure of a situation implies certain changes in the category representations associated with it, without necessarily affecting other representations associated with persisting relationships. Secord and Backman (1974) in this connection refer to the studies by Minard (1952) and Harding and Hogrefe (1952) concerning the integration of black workers in the United States. In a study of black and white miners, Minard (1952) showed that there was practically no discrimination in the mine in which Whites and Blacks worked together. Discrimination did, however, persist on the surface, where the Whites enjoyed superior status. 'The white miner adjusts to these conflicting influences by adoption of a dual role. Within the mine he assumes a role toward his fellow workers posited upon acceptance of practical equality of status. Outside his role as a member of the white community involves an elevation of status in which he becomes a member of a superior caste group' (ibid, p. 30). Integration which occurs in the work situation is not therefore necessarily carried over outside this situation.

Harding and Hogrefe (1952) come to a similar conclusion. Their study concerned the employees of a large store employing both Whites and Blacks. The attitudes studied were mainly related to relations at work, although some went beyond this. In the analysis of results, a distinction was made between Whites who had relations of equal status with Black employees in their work, and those who had no such relations, or enjoyed superior status to Blacks. The former discriminated less than the latter in respect of attitudes connected with relations at work, but there was no difference in the degree of discrimination in respect of attitudes related to situations outside work.

Field studies therefore show all the dangers of generalising results obtained in one particular situation. Like such natural situations, the experimental situation has its specific effects and its limitations. This is indicated by the findings of the experiment which we shall describe below.

There were two phases in our experimental situation. The first phase was designed to examine the functioning of category differentiation where group memberships were crossed. It was predicted that in such a situation, differentiation should be less. The second phase involved introducing a simple and pre-existing form of categorisation, in order to show that the effect of this categorisation was not modified by the experiment. Pupils aged between nine and ten years, from five classes in a primary school in a Geneva suburb were subjects in the experiment. Ten experimental groups were formed, each consisting of twelve subjects (six boys and six girls from the same class). Five of these experimental groups were assigned to a simple categorisation condition. In each group, the boys were asked to sit down on one side of the diagonal of a table, the girls on the other side. For five other groups, a cross-categorisation situation was introduced. As in the previous condition, boys and girls were placed diagonally at a table. But in addition, three boys and three girls were labelled 'red', the others 'blue'. Ball-point pens were given to the children, six red and six blue, with the remark that there was a group of reds and a group of blues. The other diagonal of the table separated these two groups.

Once the children were in position, they were asked to carry out individually certain simple paper-and-pencil tasks of the kind one finds in children's comics – mazes, dominoes, pieces to fit into a pattern, crosswords. It had previously been confirmed that these tasks did not appear to be particularly masculine or feminine. A first series served as training and the experimenter took part along with the children. Then, each child carried out alone a second series of these puzzles so that it could be judged in how many each of the twelve members of the experimental group was successful. Each was then given a score of from zero to four. For each subject, the names of the twelve members of the group were written on a response form. In the case of simple categorisation, the names of two boys and two girls were alternated; in the case of cross categorisation, the names were alternated by sex and also the names of 'red' subjects, written in red, were alternated with the names of 'blue' subjects, written in blue. The responses to this questionnaire constituted the dependent variables in the first part of the experiment.

After the end of the first part of the experiment, the children were given a second questionnaire intended to tap more general representations of their own sex membership group and of the other group. The subjects were asked to indicate, on a list of adjectives, which attributes were or were not characteristic of their own sex, and, on another identical list, those attributes which were or were not characteristic of the other sex. This list of 33 adjectives was based on interviews with children and it was previously given to a population of 25 boys and 28 girls who were asked whether it was a good thing or a bad thing to possess each quality. A very high degree of agreement enabled us to determine the evaluative connotation of each adjective (Table 19).

Table 19. *List of adjectives with their evaluative significance*

obedient	good	stunning	good
honest	good	obstinate	bad
nasty	bad	stupid	bad
quarrelsome	bad	cheerful	good
irritating	bad	brave	good
talkative	bad	comical	good
amusing	good	jealous	bad
naughty	bad	boastful	bad
aggravating	bad	timid	bad
cheating	bad	funny	good
intelligent	good	strong	good
nice	good	foolish	bad
pretty	good	simple-minded	good
kind	good	gifted	good
tell-tale	bad	afraid	bad
stingy	bad	weak	bad
sympathetic	good		

To return to the first part of the experiment, let us see whether the crossing of memberships had the predicted effect, by comparing the scores attributed by the children in the two experimental conditions. In the case of simple categorisation, there is a difference between attributions made to one's own category and those made to the other category. This difference no longer appears in the case of crossed categorisation (Table 20). In this case, there is also no differentiation in respect of the colour categories. The crossing of category memberships thus does seem to offset the differentiation effect.

Table 20. *Mean estimation of performance of others*

	Simple categorisation			Crossed categorisation		
	Boys	Girls	Total	Boys	Girls	Total
Boys	3.19	2.66	2.93	3.20	3.18	3.19
Girls	3.18	3.32	3.25	3.21	3.19	3.20

Significant Fs in the analysis of variance:
    same sex, opposite sex 10.70, d.f. $= 1$, 116, $p < 0.01$;
    same sex, opposite sex $\times$ experimental conditions 10.70, d.f. $= 1$, 116, $p < 0.01$;
    same sex, opposite sex $\times$ sex of subjects 4.61, d.f. 1, 116, $p < 0.05$.

It is a commonplace to say that the two sexes do not enjoy equal status in our societies. This difference shows in our experimental attributions. The boys differentiate more between the attributions they make to the two groups than the girls, but again, this finding is specific to the simple categorisation condition and does not appear in the other condition (Table 20). This confirms that the dynamics specific to even an experimental situation may outweigh determining factors from outside.

Let us now see whether the experimental conditions affected the more general representations covered by the lists of adjectives in the second part of the experiment. The indications are that, as predicted, this was not the case. Analysis was in terms of the number of positive and negative adjectives attributed to the two sexes. Figure 10 presents the findings. Boys and girls attribute significantly more positive adjectives and fewer negative adjectives to their own category than to the other category. The experimental conditions have practically no effect on these attributions. On the other hand, 'sociological' asymmetry tends to appear in both conditions. Girls attribute to boys more positive adjectives and fewer negative adjectives than they themselves receive.

To conclude, a particular experimental situation modifies the representations which are relevant to it according to the

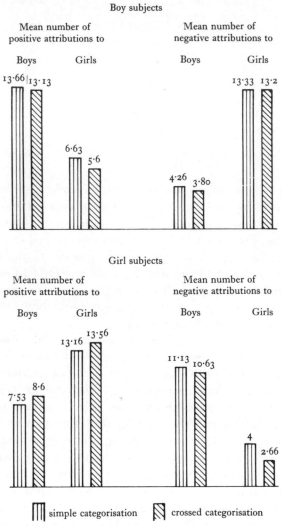

Figure 10. Mean numbers of positive and negative traits ascribed to boys and girls by subjects of different experimental conditions.

laws of the category differentiation process. The operation of the process at a specific level does not, however, affect the dynamics of its operation at a different level, that concerned with the more permanent location of subjects in the social system. The present study has thus clarified two limitations to category differentiation, one concerning its operation when category memberships are crossed, the other concerning the unique nature of a particular situation, the effects of which are not necessarily reflected through the whole system of social relations.

LINGUISTIC DIVERGENCE AND CONVERGENCE

If there is a form of behaviour deriving from the integration of psychological and sociological, it is linguistic behaviour. It is renewed in every social situation, responding to the structure of the situation but at the same time having its own system of rules. It is not our intention here to try to show how different category differentiations operate at different semantic and paradigmatic levels. We shall be concerned with differentiation of another kind, more directly related to social differentiation, i.e. differentiation in terms of regional accent.

An individual changes his accent according to the situation in which he is talking. Giles (1973) has made a special study of the way in which an individual adapts his accent to that of his partner. A person adapts his accent when he is addressing someone of superior status. This adaptation may be by way of either convergence or divergence. In the former case, the speaker approaches his partner, in the latter case he 'accentuates' the difference between himself and the other.

Anthropological findings again suggest that linguistic divergences and convergences occur according to the category differentiation model. According to Fishman (1968, p. 45), social groups minimise or exaggerate the difference between their languages according to the relations existing between them.

Divisiveness is an ideologized position and it can magnify minor differences; indeed, it can manufacture differences in languages as in other matters almost as easily as it can capitalize on more obvious differences. Similarly, unification is also an ideological position and it can minimize seemingly major differences or ignore them entirely, whether these be in the realm of language, religion, culture, race, or any other basis of differentiation.

Moscovici (1972, p. 331) in a similar way relates linguistic differentiation to his 'natural division'.

From its origins an instrument of communication and co-operation, language has also provided a means of not communicating and of creating distance. The proliferation of dialects, syntaxes, semantic fields, physical channels of transmission, signs, the imposition of double and treble meanings all reflect the wish to remain within oneself, to introduce the incomprehensible and the different into the world of the comprehensible and the commonly accepted. It may be that men started to talk in order to deceive animals, and learned to write in order to deceive those who talked.

The nature of the relations between groups must be of great importance in relation to the facility or difficulty with which members understand or learn each other's language. There is a kind of assymmetry in this field as well. Convergence and the perceptual reduction of differences occur more readily in those who occupy inferior status, while divergence and accentuation of differences occur more readily in those who occupy superior status. It is, however, clear that phenomena of this kind have a complex background. Experiment may serve to clarify the issue.

We can make the basic hypothesis that divergence and convergence at the behavioural level will also be reflected at the linguistic level. Thus, co-operation should have the effect of making more similar the accents of two partners speaking neighbouring regional dialects, while competition should increase the difference in accent. It should follow that the evaluation of situations as co-operative or competitive should vary accordingly as the accents of those concerned diverge or converge. We were fortunately able to test this hypothesis experimentally (Doise, Sinclair and Bourhis, 1976).

The experiment was concerned with the impressions retained by subjects after they had listened to a recording of a sequence of interaction between two men with different local accents. Four different interactions were presented. (1) The two persons collaborated and their accents were similar. (2) They collaborated but their accents were different. (3) They competed with one another and their accents were different. (4) They competed with one another but their accents were similar. In terms of our model, situations 1 and 3 were congruent and should therefore have been regarded by the subjects as more natural, while the other two situations, which were not congruent, should have looked odd to the subjects.

In this kind of situation, membership of a regional group on the part of the stimulus persons must have some effect, especially when such membership is shared by the subjects. It may be predicted that subjects will judge more favourably a member of their own group as opposed to a member of another group, when the member of their own group retains his local accent, independently of the overall judgments which the subjects may make of the situation.

The situations, each of which had to be judged by a different experimental group, consisted of tape-recorded conversations between two actors, one Vaudois and the other Valaisan. Vaudois and Valaisan have typical regional accents and also have fairly clearly defined stereotypes when compared to one another.

The four recordings were made from two spoken versions of the same text, presented as a radio-game. In one version, the Vaudois and the Valaisan made their accents converge so that towards the end they resembled the typical accent of Radio Suisse Romande. In another version, the Vaudois and the Valaisan, towards the end, exaggerated the qualities of their regional accents. For each of these versions, a co-operative and a competitive alternative were presented by means of two series of interventions by the 'producer'. On one occasion, she presented the game as a co-operative one, on the other as a competitive one. Co-operation was induced by opposing the two protagonists to other pairs who were not actually present. Then, the same 'producer' presented the various questions, e.g. 'In how many countries do women have the vote?' or, 'How many banks are there in Geneva?' One single version of the questions had been agreed upon for the different versions of the game. After she had played her part, the 'producer' again emphasised the competitive or co-operative nature of the relations between the two actors. By copying and interpolating the relevant passages, the four stimulus situations were so arranged that the convergence and divergence of accents was materially the same in both co-operative and competitive situations. On each recording, the Vaudois and the Valaisan had the same amount of speaking time. They interacted for approximately four minutes. No result was provided, and in any case, no subject gave correct responses to the difficult or vague questions.

The subjects were Vaudois pupils, between the ages of 15 and 16 years, divided into 4 groups of 17 subjects each, who listened to the same recording twice. The experimenter had previously told them that the aim of the experiment was to study how one judged other persons and their relations simply from the sound of their voices.

The questionnaire, designed to tap the subjects' evaluations, consisted of three pages. On the first page, subjects had to describe the relations between the two actors on ten traits, using seven-point scales. The traits were as follows; pleasant (+), candid (+), tense, natural (+), ironical, complex, aggressive, suspicious, friendly (+), eccentric. On the other two pages, the subjects had to evaluate separately the two actors on thirteen seven-point scales in respect of the following traits; candid (+), slow, competent (+), generous (+), cold, obstinate, suspicious, ambitious, sociable (+), stable (+), intelligent (+), friendly (+), good fellow (+). These adjectives were selected on the basis of previous interviews with Valaisan and Vaudois subjects. In the analysis of results, responses to adjectives followed by a cross were scored from 1 for the response 'not at all' to 7 for the

Table 21. *Mean results on the different scales used in the experiment on differences in accent*

	Experimental situations			
	Co-operation: accents		Competition: accents	
	Divergent ($N = 17$)	Convergent ($N = 17$)	Divergent ($N = 17$)	Convergent ($N = 17$)
Description of relations between Vaudois and Valaisan (10 adjectives)	46.00 (9.29)	46.00 (7.60)	53.65 (5.30)	43.23 (9.10)
Description of Vaudois (13 adjectives)	54.94 (8.15)	50.76 (7.92)	60.82 (13.03)	56.76 (8.77)
Description of Valaisan (13 adjectives)	50.94 (8.07)	49.76 (9.00)	49.58 (12.86)	50.06 (9.05)

Standard deviation in parentheses.

response 'very much indeed', while for the other adjectives, the scoring was reversed. In each case, the results for the different scales were added.

For the evaluation of relations between the two persons, the competitive situations yielded the expected results. In these situations, divergence of accents was judged more positively than convergence. The opposite is not the case for the co-operative situations (Table 21). In this respect, the experiment fares no better than the experiment on multiple differentiation. It may be that in our co-operative situations, there were still many competitive aspects; and this would explain why divergence and convergence of accents seemed to be equally accepted.

Judgments of the actor from their canton varied as predicted. Table 21 shows that the Vaudois individual is effectively perceived more favourably when he is competitive and likewise, although to a lesser extent, when he retains his accent. This study raises an important issue, concerning the connection between representations of certain relations and representations of the different parties involved in these relations. It would appear that these two kinds of representations may vary more or less independently.

INDIVIDUAL AND GROUP ENCOUNTERS

In two of the preceding experiments we have compared a group encounter with an individual encounter. The results have, without any shadow of doubt, shown that these encounters differed. We must now try to explain the basis of these differences in more detail.

In the group encounter, the object of the judgments between the parties concerned changes. The question is whether this is the only cause of the differences between inter-individual and intergroup representations. Certain experimental findings, based on studies concerned with the description of complex stimuli, suggest that this might indeed be so. Various models have been proposed to account for the complex nature of judgments of a whole which is composed of a number of elements, and more specifically, to account for the particular characteristics of these judgments. They do not simply reflect the mean of the judgments of those items constituting the whole. To explain the shift involved, some models refer to an additive process (Anderson, 1962; Fishbein and Hunter, 1964), to differential weighting of the more extreme elements (Podell and Podell, 1963), or to a constant which acts to modify the mean (Willis, 1960). The probability of observing a certain combination of elements no doubt also influences the extremity of the judgments used to describe it.

These various attempts to account for judgments of complex stimuli are of direct concern to our interests: a group is a complex stimulus. And again, one of the studies referred to, that by Willis, has to do with judgments which might be regarded as intergroup in nature. In the first part of his

Table 22. *Mean judgments of groups of photographs*

Number of photographs	Unpleasant photographs	Pleasant photographs
1	2.15	4.15
2	2.10	4.42
3	2.04	4.71

Figures on the first line represent the mean judgments of the judges describing the photographs which composed the groups of two or three to be described by the subjects.
SOURCE: after Willis, 1960, p. 370.

experiment, 32 judges classified photographs of male and female students into nine categories, from zero to eight, according to their pleasant or unpleasant appearance. Then, other judges classified the same photographs, but grouped them in twos or threes. Willis confirmed that the mean of the two photographs regarded as rather unpleasant appeared more unpleasant when grouped than when presented separately. This was even more marked in the case of groups of three photographs. The inverse was found for the pleasant photographs; the units of three photographs were seen as more pleasant than the units of two photographs which in turn were seen as more pleasant than the mean of the photographs judged separately (Table 22). Since all the subjects judged pleasant and unpleasant photographs together, it was possible for a category differentiation process to operate more decisively in so far as more elements were characterised by the same traits. Willis's conclusions are compatible with this view. The same process also seems to be involved at a different level. Table 23 shows that the subjects, especially the boys compared with the girls, overvalued the photographs of their own sex, so that there was positive differentiation in favour of a membership group.

This shows again that intergroup judgment involves more than just the characteristics of the objects of judgment.

Table 23. *Mean judgments of female and male photographs*

Sex of subjects	Male photographs	Female photographs
Male	3.48	3.21
Female	3.20	3.32

SOURCE: after Willis, 1960, p. 370.

In his experiment, Willis also got one subject or two subjects of the same sex to judge the same combinations of photographs. What he was concerned with in this manipulation was not, however, the same kind of thing as that with which we were ourselves concerned in our study of the differences between individual and group encounters. In our view, a group encounter should accentuate the degree of differentiation and then lead to definite polarisation. Willis (1960, p. 366) was concerned to show that two subjects moderated their judgments and thus differentiated less between the different combinations of photographs. His results failed to confirm his expectations, but as published they do not enable us to conclude, either, that pairs of subjects differentiated more between the different combinations than subjects in isolation.

Analysis in terms of convergence toward a member of one's own group, as we proposed in the case of the experiment with the apprentices and Genevan students, does, however, enable us to predict an intensification in evaluative differentiation when two subjects of the same sex are confronted with two photographs of members of the opposite sex. Within the framework of the category differentiation model, this introduction of a convergence effect does not represent recourse to a *deus ex machina*. Although the notion is a descriptive one as presented in the studies on group judgments, it becomes a theoretical one when it is associated with category differentiation; convergence is a result of the accentuation of intra-category similarities. Two persons converge only when, in one way or another, they identify themselves as members of one category opposed to another category.

A group encounter should differ from an individual encounter because, in the former, category differentiation in terms of social memberships is easier. In this way we can explain the differences observed between encounters involving two individuals and two groups of individuals belonging in each case to different categories. Our analysis would receive further support if we could show that a single member of a group does not react in the same way as two members of this group with respect to the same representatives of the other group. Faced with the same stimulus, for example two members of the other group, a single individual can still define the situation in different ways; this becomes more difficult when another member of his own group is present. In the latter case, the common membership will bring the categorisation process to bear on clearly defined dimensions associated with the two memberships represented. Evaluative discrimination should therefore be more significant when two members of one group are confronted with two of another group than when a single member is confronted with the same members of the other group.

A study carried out in collaboration with J.-C. Giroud was designed to test this prediction. The subjects were 36 girls and 36 boys of about 10 years of age. The experimental material consisted of three photographs of boys and three photographs of girls. In the individual situation, each subject was questioned alone. He was asked to describe the photographs of the opposite sex, one photograph by itself and the other two together (N = 12 girls and 12 boys). The three combinations of one photograph and two photographs were each described by four subjects, one half of whom began by describing a single photograph while the other half began by describing a combination of two photographs. In the group situation, two children were, for each trial, required to agree on their descriptions of the same arrangements of stimuli (N = 12 pairs of girls and 12 pairs of boys). The descriptions were made in terms of the list of adjectives already used in the second part of the experiment on crossed membership (cf. Table 19).

The experiment was thus intended to show that two subjects will evaluate less favourably the representatives of the other sex than one subject alone. This was found to be the case. The pairs of subjects gave a less favourable description than the single subjects of two photographs presented together. When the stimulus object was only a single photograph, this difference did not seem to operate (Table 24). In a way, the category membership of the other who has to be described must be shared for the difference introduced at subject level to operate.

Table 24. *Medians of evaluative indices for the description of one photograph and two photographs of members of the opposite sex*

	Sex of subjects	1 photograph	2 photographs
Individual situation	Female	0.0	+5.5
	Male	+1.0	+5.0
Group situation	Female	+2.0	+1.5
	Male	−2.5	+1.0

The index was found by calculating the difference between the number of positive adjectives and the number of negative adjectives attributed. Median test for the comparison between individual and group situations for the description of one photograph, $\chi^2 = 0.333$ (N.S.); for the description of two photographs, $\chi^2 = 4.090$; d.f. = 1, $p < 0.05$.

The experimental situation which we have just described is a very particular one. There may have been an element of sexual attraction more strongly involved when a girl or a boy was alone before the photographs of the opposite sex. But if such a factor did have any effect, it should have operated also in the case of the presentation of a single photograph; but in this case, the difference between the individual situation and the group situation no longer appears and the single photographs are not perceived as more attractive than the pairs of photographs.

This new experiment, like that with the apprentices and the students and that on the dynamics of a masculine ideology, thus shows that individuals alone do not arrive at the same definition of an encounter with the representatives of another category, as a pair of individuals. The findings as a whole suggest that in the former case an approach is made in the direction of the others and that in the latter case the situation is more defined in terms of social differentiation. Groups more easily reach a sociological definition while individuals tend to adopt a more psychological definition. A further study was designed to confirm this difference between individual encounter and group encounter, in a different situation. In fact, we set out to compare the conception of the doctor–patient relationship indicated by patients individually or in groups before a member of the medical profession. Once again, the main experimental manipulation concerned the difference between judgments made by a subject alone and those made by two subjects. In accordance with the hypothesis that an individual is more inclined to seek a psychological rapprochement with a representative of another category, we predicted that individuals alone would attach more importance to a 'psychological' conception of medical treatment. Pairs, on the other hand, would lay more emphasis on the 'scientific' or 'technical', 'less personal' aspects of the doctor–patient relationship.

Patients (38 men and 38 women) in a Geneva hospital took part in the experiment. Their mean age was 51 years and 2 months. They were given a forced choice questionnaire of ten items (Table 25). There were two experimental conditions. In the individual condition, 17 male patients and 17 female patients answered the questionnaire individually, in the absence of other patients. The questionnaire was presented to them as investigating opinions. The interviewer was an advanced medical student, dressed like a doctor. In

Table 25 – Questionnaire

Make a cross in the box corresponding to your choice for each question.

1. Would you rather be treated by a doctor
   whom you know?
   whom you don't know?

2. Would you rather go to a well-known specialist?
   or to your family doctor?

3. Would you have more confidence in a doctor who was
   intellectual but cold in manner?
   easy-going but sympathetic?

4. Would you want the doctor to be more concerned
   with your private life, even with regard to things   yes
   without direct relevance to your illness?   no

5. At the hospital, would you rather have
   the same doctor all the time?
   a number of different doctors?

6. At the hospital, would you prefer
   the staff to pay more attention to you?
   people to leave you alone?

7. Do you think it is better to be seen by
   one doctor at a time?
   several doctors at the same time?

8. When you see a doctor, would you rather
   tell him about your illness?
   have him question you on a standardised
   questionnaire?

9. Would you want the doctor to explain your illness to
   you in as detailed a way as possible?   yes
                                            no

10. Would you prefer
    a very polite doctor with perhaps too much discretion?
    a very straightforward doctor with an abrupt manner?

The score is obtained by counting the number of responses which fall in the squares marked with a cross.

the group condition, seven groups of three male patients and seven groups of three female patients were asked to answer the same questionnaire. The experimenter asked them to give an agreed response to each question, or if that was not possible, to give a majority response.

Table 26. *Mean scores on the medical treatment questionnaire*

Subjects	Individual condition	Group condition
Men	5.74 ($N = 17$)	4.14 ($N = 7$)
Women	7.11 ($N = 17$)	6.71 ($n = 7$)

F for analysis of variance: experimental conditions 4.370, d.f. = 1, 44, $p < 0.05$; sex 10.940, d.f. = 1, 44, $p < 0.01$; interaction 1.252, d.f = 1, 44, N.S.

The results show that individuals prefer a more 'personal' form of medical care than groups. This finding supports our hypothesis. It is however, largely due to the responses of the men. Accordingly, we can only conclude that individual encounter and group encounter differ in this situation when a difference in sex is not involved. Moreover, in the two experimental conditions the female subjects, confronted with a young male doctor, preferred a personal form of medical care to a greater extent than the male subjects. As distinct from the experiment with the photographs, the predicted effect was found when there was only a single representative of the other category. It is true that the context and the role of the interviewer in the hospital made his membership of the medical staff highly significant. All in all, we may note that the results concerning the difference between individual and group encounters cannot be explained in terms of group polarisation (Doise and Moscovici, 1972). Instead of increasing the tendency shown by the individual responses, group interaction actually lessened it. The effects studied here seem more powerful than those caused by group polarisation. Moreover, it is not impossible that this very polarisation, which only appears when there is initial divergence between individual responses (Moscovici, Doise and Dulong, 1972), is itself a result of category differentiation. Polarisation might be the result of differentiation within a discussion group in which one side wins.

INTRA-CATEGORY SIMILARITIES

In the different conditions of the experiments reported, differentiations between groups become more or less marked according to the category differentiation model. But what about the other aspect of categorisation, the accentuation of similarities between members of the same class? Whenever it has been shown that convergence towards the members of their own group was necessary for subjects to discriminate with respect to the members of another group, there has been the implication of a relationship between intra-group cohesiveness and differentiation between groups. It has not, however, been demonstrated so far that category differentiation is associated with accentuation of intra-category similarities. Two experiments were therefore carried out to demonstrate such an association. Unlike the experiment of Tajfel, Sheikh and Gardner (1964), to which we have already referred, they indicate that the accentuation of intra-category similarities is a result of the categorisation process and not just a 'realistic' registration of social facts.

The first of these experiments was carried out in collaboration with J.-C. Deschamps. The experimental manipulation was analogous to one of the manipulations in the experiment with the apprentices and students. In the first condition (no anticipation), subjects were asked to describe the members of a group without being told that they would also be asked to describe the members of another group. In the second condition (with anticipation), the subjects, asked to describe the members of the first group, were told that they would also have to describe the members of the other group. The experimental predictions were that intra-category similarities and inter-category differences would be more marked in the anticipation condition than in the no anticipation condition.

The subjects were 72 girls and 72 boys, of approximately 10 years of age. The experimental material consisted of three photographs of boys and three photographs of girls which had already been used in the experiment carried out with J.-C. Giroud on individual and group encounters. The subjects' task was to indicate, for each photograph, which of 24 adjectives in a list adapted from that in Table 19, were suitable to describe the child shown on the photograph. But although all the subjects described six photographs on six lists in this way, three photographs only, belonging to the same sex category, were presented from the start to half of them (no anticipation condition) while all the photographs were presented from the start to the other half of the subjects (with anticipation condition). The order of description of the six photographs was determined so that one half of the boys and girls began by describing, in a fixed order, the three photographs of members of their own sex, while the other half began by describing three photographs of members of the other sex. The subjects took part in the experiment in groups of six, of the same sex.

The results are given in Tables 27 and 28. The differentiation index, which sums for all subjects the absolute differences between the number of times a trait has been attributed to the three photographs of girls and the number of times it has been attributed to the three photographs of boys, confirms the findings of the experiment with the apprentices and students. Differentiation is greater when there is reference to the other group from the beginning of the experiment and the boys, as members of the socially dominant group, differentiate more than the girls, especially when confronted with the other group, as anticipated.

The accentuation of intra-category similarities accompanies inter-category differentiation. The number of times a

Table 27. *Mean differences between categories in the description of six photographs*

Subjects	No anticipation condition	Anticipation condition
Girls	18.66	22.16
Boys	21.41	27.02

Significant results of analysis of variance: boys/girls, $F = 16.21$, d.f. $= 1$, 140, $p < 0.0001$; anticipation: 11.31, d.f. $= 1$, 140, $p < 0.001$.

Table 28. *Means of intra-category similarity scores for descriptions of six photographs*

Subjects	Descriptions of photographs of girls		Descriptions of photographs of boys	
	No anticipation	Anticipation	No anticipation	Anticipation
Girls	9.61	11.83	9.08	11.33
Boys	6.66	12.02	8.55	11.27

Significant results of analysis of variance: anticipation – $F = 29.70$, d.f. $= 1$, 140, $p < 0.0001$.

subject attributes the same trait to all the three photographs of the same category is significantly higher when, from the start, the subjects anticipate the description of members of another category. The accentuation of intra-category similarities therefore appears to be associated with category differentiation.

With the collaboration of G. Meyer, we were again able to vary intra-category similarities in accordance with the category differentiation model. It is well-known that Switzerland comprises three linguistic groups: German speaking, French speaking and Italian speaking. The latter two groups are not only distinguished from the first as 'Latin' minority groups, they are also frequently regarded as economically less active. As in other countries, 'Latin' people are distinguished from 'Germanic' people in Switzerland (Doise, 1969b). Nevertheless, we should expect the differences between French Swiss or Italian Swiss on the one hand and German Swiss on the other hand to vary according to the categorisation process. These differences should be less when the two Swiss groups are confronted with a group of non-Swiss.

The subjects, pupils of the 'cycle d'orientation' at Geneva and of approximately 14 years of age, answered a questionnaire which asked them to describe three social groups on 16 eight-point scales. According to the experimental conditions, these groups were German Swiss, French Swiss and Italian Swiss (control condition) or two of these groups to which were added Germans from Germany, French from France and Italians from Italy, who replaced respectively the German Swiss, the French Swiss and the Italian Swiss (experimental conditions). The four questionnaires were mixed and distributed to the students during a lecture. Answering the questionnaire was anonymous, but the last page, which was concerned with sociological aspects, enabled us to isolate the questionnaires completed by students of foreign origin.

Experiment in this field was difficult in Geneva, only a few weeks after the referendum on foreigners at the end of 1974. Particular care was therefore taken in framing the experimental questionnaire (Table 29). In fact each scale contrasted poles of a similar evaluation but of an opposed descriptively 'tight' or 'loose' connotation (Peabody, 1968). The subjects had to place the three letters symbolising the groups which they had to describe on the eight points of each scale. The instructions indicated that they could put two or three letters together, if there were no differences between certain groups or between all the groups described.

The number of points which the subjects left between two Swiss groups constituted the dependent variables. These numbers were added across the 16 scales. The means, given

Table 29. *Scales used for the description of different Swiss and non-Swiss groups*

1. thrifty	extravagant	9. obstinate	uncertain
2. serious	merry	10. energetic	quiet
3. sceptical	trusting	11. tactful	direct
4. strict	negligent	12. aggressive	submissive
5. inhibited	impulsive	13. timid	rash
6. restless	calm	14. prudent	brave
7. stubborn	flexible	15. lacking	showy
8. miserly	spendthrift	self-assurance	
		16. active	idle

Table 30. *Mean perceived differences between regional Swiss groups*

Differences between	Condition without foreign group ($N = 42$)	Condition with foreign group ($N = 45, 45, 47$)	t one-tailed test
German–Italian Swiss	48.90 (18.76)	41.07 (12.96)	2.30 $p < 0.02$
German–French Swiss	45.86 (18.71)	39.00 (14.05)	1.97 $p < 0.03$
French–Italian Swiss	42.07 (16.99)	42.28 (15.73)	0.06

Standard deviation in parentheses.

in Table 30, confirm that the differences between French Swiss and German Swiss or between Italian Swiss and German Swiss are less important when these groups are described along with a non-Swiss group. Such a lessening of effect does not appear in respect of differences between Italian Swiss and French Swiss. Among Swiss groups, they appear more similar as 'Latin' groups, opposed to the 'Germanic' group.

Category differentiation can account for the way in which the ideological effect of the division into categories finds expression at the social psychological level. The two studies on intra-category similarities show that the same process accounts for the social psychological basis for certain intra-category integrations which may well be compared with the ideological aspects of the Holy Alliance, concealing the internal contradictions within any one social system when nations confront one another.

In intergroup relations, as in other fields of human behaviour, psychological and sociological explanations complement one another in social psychological explanation. This position has been abundantly justified in the present book in relation to intergroup relations. Psychologists study the individual bases for these relations. They do not study how the behaviour, evaluation and representations of individuals depend on social relations. Sociologists study the relations between groups or classes without clarifying the way in which they evolve from individual bases. Experiment offers a particularly appropriate means of integrating these two approaches. The exploratory studies which we have reported in the first part of this book also show the relevance of such integration for the study of cognitive development. The psychological aspect of this development has already been the subject of detailed investigation, and there are currently numerous controversies concerning the sociological and ethnological factors by which it is conditioned. Consequently, the development of a social psychology of cognitive development is becoming of particular importance. It is our intention to continue in this direction the exploration of the field to which the present book has been devoted.

Bibliography

English translations are cited where available.

Adorno, T. W., Frenkel-Brunswick, E., Levinson, D. J., and Sanford, R. N. 1950. *The Authoritarian Personality.* N.Y., Harper.

Althusser, L. 1969. *For Marx.* London, Allen Lane.

Althusser, L. 1970. Idéologie et appareils idéologiquies d'état. *La Pensée*, **151**, 3–38.

Althusser, L. 1973. *Réponse à John Lewis.* Paris, Maspero.

Anderson, N. H. 1962. Application of an additive model to impression formation. *Science*, **138**, 817–18.

Avigdor, R. 1953. Étude expérimentale de la genèse des stéréotypes. *Cahiers Internationaux de Sociologie*, **14**, 154–68.

Bandura, A. and Walters, R. H. 1963. *Social Learning and Personality Development.* N.Y., Holt.

Bass, B. M. 1965. *Personal Background and Intergroup Competitiveness.* Technical Report 7, Contract N.O.N.R., 624 (14).

Bass, B. M. and Dunteman, G. 1963. Biases in the evaluation of one's own group, its allies and opponents. *Journal of Conflict Resolution*, **7**, 16–20.

Beals, A. R. 1962. Pervasive factionalism in a South Indian village. In M. Sherif (ed.), *Intergroup Relations and Leadership*, N.Y., Wiley, 247–66.

Berkowitz, L. 1965. The concept of aggressive drive; some additional considerations. In L. Berkowitz (ed.), *Advances in Experimental Social Psychology.* N.Y. and London, Academic Press, II, 301–29.

Berkowitz, L. and Geen, R. G. 1966. Film violence and the cue properties of available targets. *J. pers. soc. Psychol.*, **3**, 525–30.

Billig, M. and Tajfel, H. 1973. Social categorization and similarity in intergroup behaviour. *European Journal of Social Psychology*, **3**, 27–52.

Blake, R. R. and Mouton, J. S. 1961. Comprehension of own and

210

of out-group positions under intergroup competition. *Journal of Conflict Resolution*, **5**, 304–10.

Blake, R. R. and Mouton, J. S. 1962. Comprehension of points of communality in competing solutions. *Sociometry*, **25**, 56–63.

Blake, R. R. and Mouton, J. S. 1962b. Overevaluation of own group's product in intergroup competitions. *J. abnorm. soc. Psychol.*, **64**, 237–8.

Brehm, J. W. 1966. *A Theory of Psychological Reactance*. N.Y., Academic Press.

Brown, R. 1965. *Social Psychology*. N.Y., The Free Press.

Bruner, J. S. 1957. On perceptual readiness. *Psychol. Rev.*, **64**, 123–52.

Bruner, J. S. and Goodman, C. C. 1947. Value and need as organizing factors in perception. *J. abnorm. soc. Psychol.*, **42**, 33–44.

Bruner, J. S. and Perlmutter, H. V. 1957. Compatriot and foreigner: A study of impression formation in three countries. *J. abnorm. soc. Psychol.*, **55**, 253–60.

Campbell, D. T. 1967. Stereotypes and the perception of group differences. *American Psychologist*, **22**, 817–29.

Chance, N. A. 1962. Factionalism as a process of social and cultural change. In M. Sherif (ed.), *Intergroup Relations and Leadership*. N.Y., Wiley, 267–73.

Chombart de Lauwe, M. J., Huguet, M., Perroy, E. and Bisseret, N. 1967. *La Femme dans la Société*. Paris, Centre National de la Recherche Scientifique.

Clarke, R. B. and Campbell, D. T. 1955. A demonstration of bias in estimates of negro ability. *J. abnorm. soc. Psychol.*, **51**, 585–8.

Dann, H. D. and Doise, W. 1974. Ein neuer methodologischer Ansatz zur experimentellen Erforschung von Intergruppen-Beziehungen. *Zeitschrift für Socialpsychologie*, **5**, 2–15.

Deconchy, J. P. 1971. *L'orthodoxie religieuse. Essai de logique psycho-sociale*. Paris, Editions Ouvrières.

Deschamps, J. C. 1975. 'L'attribution et la catégorisation sociale'. Thesis, University of Paris.

Deschamps, J. C. and Doise, W. 1974. 'Attribution intersexes dans des conditions de catégorisation simple et de catégorisation croisés.' Geneva, Faculté de Psychologie.

Devereux, G. 1961. Two types of modal personality models. In B. Kaplan (ed.), *Studying Personality Cross-culturally*. Evanston, Ill., Row Peterson, 227–311.

Devereux, G. 1972. *Ethnopsychanalyse Complémentariste*. Paris, Flammarion.

Devereux, G. 1976. *A Study of Abortion in Primitive Societies.* Revised edition, N.Y., International Universities Press, Inc. (First edition 1955).

Diab, L. N. 1970. A study of intragroup and intergroup relations among experimentally produced small groups. *Genetic Psychology Monographs,* **82,** 49–82.

Doise, W. 1969a. Intergroup relations and polarization of individual and collective judgments. *J. pers. soc. Psychol.,* **12,** 136–43.

Doise, W. 1969b. Autoritarisme, dogmatisme et mode d'approche des relations internationales. *Journal de Psychologie Normale et Pathologique,* **66,** 35–54.

Doise, W. 1969c. Jugement collectif et prise de risque des petits groupes. *Psychologie Française,* **14,** 87–95.

Doise, W. 1969d. Stratégies de jeu à l'intérieur et entre des groupes de nationalités différentes. *Bulletin du C.E.R.P.,* **18,** 13–26.

Doise, W. 1973. La structuration cognitive des decisions individuelles et collectives d'adultes et d'enfants. *Revue de Psychologie et des Sciences de l'Education,* **8,** 133–46.

Doise, W. 1974. Individual and collective preferences for different styles of medical care. *European Journal of Social Psychology,* **4,** 251–3.

Doise, W. Csepeli, G., Dann, H.-D., Gouge, C., Larsen, K. and Ostell, A. 1972. An experimental investigation into the formation of intergroup representations. *European Journal of Social Psychology,* **2,** 202–4.

Doise, W. and Moscovici, S. 1973. Les décisions collectives. In S. Moscovici (ed.), *Introduction à la Psychologie Sociale,* Paris, Larousse, II, 114–34.

Doise, W. and Mugny, G. 1975. Recherches socio-génétiques sur la coordination d'actions interdépendantes. *Revue Suisse de Psychologie Pure et Appliquée,* **34,** 160–74.

Doise, W., Mugny, G. and Perret-Clermont, A. N. 1975. Social interaction and the development of cognitive operations. *European Journal of Social Psychology,* **5,** 367–83.

Doise, W., Sinclair, A. and Bourhis, R. Y. 1976. Evaluation of accent convergence and divergence in competitive and cooperative intergroup situations. *British Journal of social and clinical Psychology,* **15,** 247–52.

Doise, W. and Weinberger, M. 1972–3. Représentations masculines dans différentes situations de rencontres mixtes. *Bulletin de Psychologie,* **26,** 649–57.

Dustin, D. S. and Davis, H. P. 1970. Evaluative bias in group and individual competition. *J. soc. Psychol.*, **80**, 103–8.

Eiser, J. R. 1971. Enhancement of contrast in the absolute judgment of attitude statements. *J. pers. soc. Psychol.*, **17**, 1–10.

Eiser, J. R. 1973. Judgment of attitude statements as a function of judges' attitudes and judgmental dimensions. *Brit. J. soc. clin. Psychol.*, **12**, 231–40.

Eiser, J. R. and Mower White, C. J. 1974. Evaluative consistency and social judgment. *J. pers. soc. Psychol.*, **30**, 349–59.

Eiser, J. R. and Stroebe, W. 1972. *Categorization and Social Judgment*. London, Academic Press.

Evans-Pritchard, E. E. 1940. *The Nuer*. London, Oxford University Press.

Faucheux, C. and Moscovici, S. 1960. Etude sur la créativité des groupes: II. Tâche, structure de communication et réussite. *Bulletin du C.E.R.P.*, **9**, 11–22.

Ferguson, C. K. and Kelley, H. H. 1964. Significant factors in overevaluation of own-group's product. *J. abnorm. soc. Psychol.*, **69**, 223–7.

Festinger, L. A. 1954. A theory of social comparison process. *Human Relations*, **7**, 117–40.

Fishbein, M. and Hunter, R. 1964. Summation versus balance in attitude organization and change. *J. abnorm. soc. Psychol.*, **69**, 505–10.

Fishman, J. A. 1968. Nationality-nationalism and nation-nationism. In J. A. Fishman, C. A. Ferguson and J. D. Gupta (eds.), *Language Problems of Developing Countries*. N.Y., Wiley.

French, J. R. P. 1941. The disruption and cohesion of groups. *J. abnorm. soc. Psychol.*, **36**, 361–77.

Freud, S. 1955. *The Standard Edition of the Complete Psychological Works*, XVIII. London, Hogarth Press.

Geen, R. G. and Berkowitz, L. 1966. Name-mediated aggressive cue properties. *J. Pers.*, 1966, **34**, 456–65.

Gergen, K. J. 1973. Social psychology as history. *J. pers. soc. Psychol.*, **26**, 309–20.

Giles, H. 1973. Accent mobility: A model and some data. *Anthropological Linguistics*, **15**, 87–105.

Hall, J. and Watson, W. H. 1970. The effects of a normative intervention on group decision-making performance. *Human Relations*, **23**, 299–317.

Hall, J. and Williams, M. S. 1966. A comparison of decision-making performances in established and ad hoc groups. *J. pers. soc. Psychol.*, **3**, 214–22.

Harding, J. and Hogrefe, R. 1952. Attitudes of white department store employees toward negro co-workers. *Journal of social Issues*, **8**, 18–28.

Harvey, O. J. 1956. An experimental investigation of negative and positive relations between small groups through judgmental indices. *Sociometry*, **19**, 201–9.

Herbert, T. 1966. Réflexions sur la situation théorique des sciences sociales et, spécialement de la psychologie sociale. *Cahiers pour l'analyse*, **1–2**, 141–67.

Holzkamp, K. 1972. *Kritische Psychologie*. Frankfurt am Main, Fischer Taschenbuch Verlag.

Holzkamp, K. 1973. *Sinnliche Erkentniss. Historischer Ursprung und Gesellschaftliche Funktion der Warnehmung*. Frankfurt am Main, Fischer Athenäum.

Holzkamp, K. and Schurig, V. 1973. Zur Einführung. To A. N. Leontjew, Probleme der Entwicklung des Psychischen. In A. N. Leontjew, *Probleme der Entwicklung des Psychischen*, Frankfurt am Main, Fischer Athenäum.

Inhelder, B. and Piaget, J. 1958. *The Growth of Logical Thinking from Childhood to Adolescence*. London, Routledge and Kegan Paul.

Jaulin, R. 1973. *Gens du soi, gens de l'autre*. Paris, Union Générale d'Editions.

Kephart, W. M. 1954. Negro visibility. *Amer. sociol. Rev.*, **19**, 462–7.

Kogan, N. and Wallach, M. A. 1967. Le comportement de prise de risque dans les petits groupes de décision. *Bulletin du C.E.R.P.*, **16**, 361–75.

Le Bon, G. 1896. *The Crowd. A Study of the Popular Mind*. London, Unwin.

Lemaine, G. 1966. Inegalité, comparaison et incomparabilité: Esquisse d'une théorie de l'originalité sociale. *Bulletin de Psychologie*, **20**, 1–2.

Lemaine, G. 1974. Social differentiation and social originality. *Eur. J. soc. Psychol.*, **4**, 17–52.

Lemaine, G. and Kastersztein, J. 1971–2. Recherches sur l'originalité sociale, la différenciation et l'incomparabilité. *Bulletin de Psychologie*, **25**, 673–93.

Lemaine, G., Lasch, E. and Ricateau, P. 1971–2. L'influence sociale et les systèmes d'action. Les effets d'attraction et de répulsion dans une expérience de normalisation avec l'allocinétique. *Bulletin de Psychologie*, **25**, 482–93.

Lemaine, G., Matalon, B. and Provansal, B. 1969. La lutte pour la vie dans la cité scientifique. *Revue Française de Sociologie*, **10**, 139–65.

Leontiev, A. N. 1973. *Probleme der Entwicklung des Psychischen.* Frankfurt am Main, Fischer Athenäum.

LeVine, R. A. and Campbell, D. T. 1972. *Ethnocentrism: Theories of Conflict, Ethnic Attitudes and Group Behaviour.* London, Wiley.

Lévi-Strauss, C. 1963. *Structural Anthropology.* N.Y., Basic Books.

Lévi-Strauss, C. 1969. *The Elementary Structures of Kinship.* London, Eyre and Spottiswoode.

Lewin, K. 1958. Group decision and social change. In E. Maccoby, T. Newcomb and E. Hartley (eds.), *Readings in Social Psychology.* N.Y., Holt, Rinehart, 197–211.

Lorenz, K. 1966. *On Aggression.* London, Methuen.

Lorge, I. and Solomon, H. 1955. Two models of group behaviour in the solution of eureka-type problems. *Psychometrika*, **20**, 139–48.

Lukács, G. 1971. *History and Class Consciousness: Studies in Marxist Dialectics.* London, Merlin Press.

Lysak, W. and Gilchrist, J. C. 1955. Value equivocality and goal availability. *J. Pers.*, **23**, 500–1.

Manheim, H. C. 1960. Intergroup interaction as related to status leadership differences between groups. *Sociometry*, **23**, 415–27.

Mann, J. W. 1963. Rivals of different rank. *J. soc. Psychol.*, **61**, 11–27.

Marchand, B. 1970. Auswirkung einer emotional wertvollen und einer emotional neutralen Klassifikation auf die Schätzung einer Stimulus-Serie. *Zeitschrift für Sozialpsychologie*, **1**, 264–74.

McDougall, W. 1908. *An Introduction to Social Psychology.* London, Methuen.

McDougall, W. 1920. *The Group Mind.* Cambridge University Press.

Mead, G. H. 1934. *Mind, Self and Society.* Chicago, Illinois, University of Chicago Press.

Mees, U. 1974. *Vorausurteil und aggressives Verhalten.* Stuttgart, Ernst Klett Verlag.

Minard, R. D. 1952. Race relationships in the Pocahontas coalfield. *J. soc. Issues*, **8**, 29–44.

Moscovici, S. 1968. *Essai sur l'histoire humaine de la nature.* Paris, Flammarion.

Moscovici, S. 1972. *La société contre nature.* Paris, Union Générale d'Editions.

Moscovici, S. and Doise, W. 1974. Decision making in groups. In C. Nemeth (ed.), *Social Psychology, Classic and Contemporary Integrations*. Chicago, Rand McNally, 250–87.

Moscovici, S., Doise, W. and Dulong, R. 1972. Studies in group decision II: Differences of opinion and group polarization. *Eur. J. soc. Psychol.*, **2**, 385–99.

Moscovici, S. and Zavalloni, M. 1969. The group as a polarizer of attitudes. *J. pers. soc. Psychol.*, **12**, 125–35.

Moscovici, S., Zavalloni, M. and Weinberger, M. 1972. Studies on polarization of judgments; person perception, ego involvement and group interaction. *Eur. J. soc. Psychol.*, **2**, 92–4.

Mugny, G. 1974. 'Négociations et influence minoritaire'. Geneva, Ecole de Psychologie.

Nielsen, R. F. 1951. *Le développement de la sociabilité chez l'enfant*. Neuchâtel, Delachaux et Nestlé.

Pagès, M. 1971–2. La culture de Bethel en 1969. *Bulletin de Psychologie*, **25**, 290–303.

Paicheler, G. 1974. *Normes et changements d'attitudes. De la modifications des attitudes envers les femmes*. Paris, Ecole Pratique des Hautes Etudes.

Peabody, D. 1968. Group judgments in the Phillipines; evaluative and descriptive aspects. *J. pers. soc. Psychol.*, **10**, 290–300.

Piaget, J. 1950. *The Psychology of Intelligence*. London, Routledge and Kegan Paul.

Piaget, J. 1965. *Etudes sociologiques*. Paris, Droz, 1965.

Piaget, J. 1969. *The Mechanisms of Perception*. London, Routledge and Kegan Paul.

Piaget, J. 1971. *Biology and Knowledge*. Edinburgh University Press.

Piaget, J. and Inhelder, B. 1956. *The Child's Conception of Space*. London, Routledge and Kegan Paul.

Piaget, J. and Inhelder, B. 1971. *Mental Imagery in the Child*. London, Routledge and Kegan Paul.

Piaget, J. and Weil, A. M. 1951. Le développement chez l'enfant, de l'idée de patrie et des relations avec l'étranger. *Bulletin International des Sciences Sociales*, Paris, UNESCO, **3**, 605–21.

Podell, H. A. and Podell, J. E. 1963. Quantitative connotation of a concept. *J. abnorm. soc. Psychol.*, **67**, 509–13.

Poulantzas, N. 1973. *Political Power and Social Classes*. London, NLB.

Poulantzas, N. 1974. *Fascism and Dictatorships*. London, NLB.

Preiswerk, R. and Perret, D. 1975. *Ethnocentrisme et Histoire*. Paris, Editions Anthropos.

Rabbie, J. M. and Horwitz, M. 1969. The arousal of ingroup–outgroup bias by a chance win or loss. *J. pers. soc. Psychol.*, **13**, 269–77.

Rabbie, J. M. and Wilkens, G. 1971. Intergroup competition and its effect on intragroup and intergroup relations. *Eur. J. soc. Psychol.*, **1**, 215–34.

Razran, G. 1950. Ethnic dislikes and stereotypes: A laboratory study. *J. abnorm. soc. Psychol.*, **45**, 7–27.

Rex, J. 1969. Race as a social category. *Journal of Biosocial Science*, Supp. No. 1, 145–52.

Roberts, M. D. 1967. 'The persistence of interpersonal trust'. Master's thesis, University of Connecticut.

Rocheblave-Spenlé, A. M. 1964. *Les roles masculins et feminins*. Paris, Presses Universitaires de France.

Rokeach, M. 1960. *The Open and Closed Mind: A Study of Belief and Disbelief Systems*. N.Y., Basic Books.

Rotter, J. B. 1967. A new scale for the measurement of interpersonal trust. *J. Pers.*, **35**, 651–65.

Rotter, J. B. 1971. Generalized expectancies for interpersonal trust. *Amer. Psychol.*, **26**, 443–52.

Roudinesco, E. 1973. *Un discours au réel*. Paris, Mâme.

Sampson, S. F. 1968. 'Crisis in the cloisters: A sociological analysis'. Ph.D. Thesis, Cornell University.

Sebag, L. 1964. *Marxisme et Structuralisme*. Paris, Payot.

Secord, P. F. and Backman, C. W. 1974. *Social Psychology*. N.Y., McGraw Hill.

Sellitz, G., Edrich, H. and Cook, S. W. 1965. Ratings of favourableness of statements about a social group as an indicator of attitudes towards the group. *J. pers. soc. Psychol.*, **2**, 408–15.

Sherif, M. 1935. A study of some social factors in perception. *Archives of Psychology*, no. 187.

Sherif, M. 1951. Experimental study of intergroup relations. In J. H. Rohrer and M. Sherif (eds.). *Social Psychology at the Crossroads*. N.Y., Harper & Row, 388–426.

Sherif, M. 1954. Integrating field work and laboratory in small group research, *American Sociological Review*, **19**, 759–71.

Sherif, M. and C. 1969. *Social Psychology*. N.Y., Harper & Row.

Sherif, M., Harvey, O. J., White, B. J., Hood, W. R. and Sherif, C. W. 1961. *Intergroup Conflict and Co-operation. The Robbers' Cave Experiment*. Norman, Okla., University Book Exchange.

Smedslund, J. 1966. Les origines sociales de la décentration. In *Psychologie et Epistémologie. Thèmes piagétiens*. Paris, Dunod, 159–67.

Smith, M. B., Bruner, J. S. and White, R. W. 1956. *Opinions and Personality*. N.Y., Wiley.

Suttles, G. D. 1972. *The Social Construction of Communities*. Chicago, University of Chicago Press.

Tajfel, H. 1959. Quantitative judgment in social perception. *Brit. J. Psychol.*, **50**, 16–29.

Tajfel, H. 1969. Social and cultural factors in perception. In G. Lindzey and E. Aronson, *Handbook of Social Psychology*, 2nd edition, III, 315–94.

Tajfel, H. 1970. Experiments in intergroup discrimination. *Scientific American*, **223**, 96–102.

Tajfel, H. 1972. La catégorisation sociale. In S. Moscovici (ed.), *Introduction à la psychologie sociale*, Paris, Larousse, I, 272–302.

Tajfel, H., Billig, M., Bundy, R. P. and Flament, C. 1971. Social categorization and intergroup behaviour. *Eur. J. soc. Psychol.*, **1**, 149–78.

Tajfel, H., Sheikh, A. A. and Gardner, R. C. 1964. Content of stereotypes and the inference of similarity between members of stereotyped groups. *Acta Psychologica*, **22**, 191–201.

Tajfel, H. and Wilkes, A. L. 1963. Classification and quantitative judgment. *Brit. J. Psychol.*, **54**, 101–14.

Thion, S. 1969. *Le pouvoir pâle ou le racisme Sud-Africain*. Paris, Editions du Seuil.

Thurstone, L. L. and Chave, E. J. 1929. *The Measurement of Attitudes*. Chicago, University of Chicago Press.

Turner, J. 1972. 'Competition between self and others, with and without categorization into groups'. Bristol, Department of Psychology.

Turner, J. 1975. Social comparison and social identity: Some prospects for intergroup behaviour. *Eur. J. soc. Psychol.*, **5**, 5–34.

Vidal, D. 1971. *Essai sur l'idéologie*. Paris, Anthropos.

Von Rad, G. 1960. *Theologie des alten Testaments*. München, C. Kaiser.

Willis, R. H. 1960. Stimulus pooling and social perception. *J. abnorm. soc. Psychol.*, **60**, 365–73.

Wilson, W., Chun, N. and Kayatani, M. 1965. Projection, attraction and strategy choices in intergroup competition. *J. pers. soc. Psychol.*, **2**, 432–5.

Wilson, W. and Kayatani, M. 1968. Intergroup attitudes and strategies in games between opponents of the same or of a different race. *J. pers. soc. Psychol.*, **9**, 24–30.

Zavalloni, M. and Cook, S. W. 1965. Influence of judges' attitudes on ratings of favourableness of statements about a social group. *J. pers. soc. Psychol.*, **1**, 43–54.

Zimbardo, P. G. 1969. The human choice: Individuation, reason and order versus deindividuation, impulse, and chaos. In W. J. Arnold and D. Levine (eds.), *Nebraska Symposium on Motivation*. Lincoln, Nebraska, University of Nebraska Press, 237–307.

Index